Copyright © 2014, 2005, 1997 PAGODA Academy, Inc.

All rights reserved. No part of this publication may be reproduced, stored in a retrieval system, or transmitted, in any form, or by any means, electronic, mechanical, photocopying, recording, or otherwise, without the prior written permission of the copyright holder and the publisher.

Published by PAGODA Books
PAGODA Books is the professional language publishing company of the PAGODA Education Group.
19F, PAGODA Tower, 419, Gangnam-daero,
Seocho-gu, Seoul, 06614, Rep. of KOREA
www.pagodabook.com

First published 2014
Tenth impression 2025
Printed in the Republic of Korea

ISBN 978-89-6281-505-4 (13740)

Publisher	Kyung-Sil Park
Writers	Lee Robinson, Ben Huber, Judson Wright, Nathan Morris
Editor	Dayna Garwacki
Advisor	Ruda Go
Illustrator	Dae Ho Kim

Acknowledgements
Sang Hee Kang, Michael Cardoza, Ji Young Kim, Lionel Ouellette, Song Rim Park, and Gemma Young for production and support
Nathan Morris, Chris Jack, and Chris Patton for trialing and feedback
Lionel Ouellette, Dayna Garwacki, Michael Cardoza, and Gemma Young for voice recording

A defective book may be exchanged at the store where you purchased it.

To Our Students

The SLE program is a conversation program for adult and young adult students who want to improve their English in an enjoyable, effective, and authentic way. It allows students to use English in a variety of contexts with an emphasis on many different useful functions. Our goal is to improve your confidence in your speaking, listening, reading, and writing ability while improving your vocabulary and grammar skills. We will help you to understand not only the "How" but the "Why" of English usage.

The SLE Level 1 textbook series is meant for students with a general understanding of the basics of English conversation skills. The material in this book focuses on building students' ability to perform basic functions and use essential structures.

Contents SLE 1C

To Our Students | 3
Format of the Book | 6
Goals for the Course | 7
Meet the Jones Family | 8

UNIT 1
Been There, Done That
Introductions & Experiences
▶ 11

LESSON 1 | 12
LESSON 2 | 20

UNIT 2
Tailor Made
Politeness & Description
▶ 31

LESSON 1 | 32
LESSON 2 | 40

UNIT 3
Look Before You Leap
Safety & Prohibition
▶ 51

LESSON 1 | 52
LESSON 2 | 60

UNIT 4
It Takes All Kinds!
Impressions & Connections
▶ 69

LESSON 1 | 70
LESSON 2 | 76

UNIT 5
X Marks The Spot
Location & Transportation
▶ 87

LESSON 1 | 88
LESSON 2 | 94

Listening Dialogues | 192
Glossary | 197

UNIT 6
I'm Glad You Asked
Reporting & Connecting
▶ **107**

| LESSON 1 | 108 |
| LESSON 2 | 114 |

UNIT 7
The Real World
Existence & Speculation
▶ **123**

| LESSON 1 | 124 |
| LESSON 2 | 132 |

UNIT 8
Occupational Hazard
Preference & Duration
▶ **143**

| LESSON 1 | 144 |
| LESSON 2 | 152 |

UNIT 9
Once Upon A Time
Morals & Anecdotes
▶ **161**

| LESSON 1 | 162 |
| LESSON 2 | 168 |

UNIT 10
Looking Back
Bringing It All Together
▶ **179**

| LESSON 1 | 180 |

Format of the Book:

Overall Format >
There are ten units in this textbook, each with its own focus. In each unit there are two individual lessons. The focus of the lesson is either grammatical or topical. Each unit consists of the following elements:

Warm Up >
The warm up for each lesson has its own purpose. The lesson one warm up is used as an opportunity to start thinking about the topic and includes functional language such as idioms, collocations, and tongue twisters that relate to the topic as a whole. The lesson two warm up is used as a quick review of the language used in the first lesson and a bridge to the second lesson.

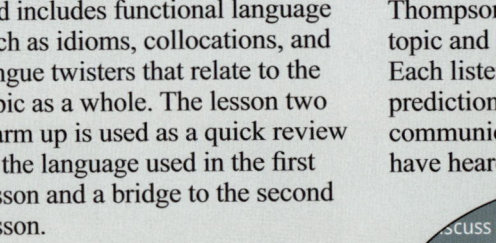

Listening >
Each listening follows the story of the Thompson family and relates to the unit topic and language points used in that unit. Each listening requires the student to make predictions based on illustrations and use communicative language to discuss what they have heard.

Language Point >
Language points occur at the start of any activity where a specific grammar or function point is used in that activity and needs to be explained to the student.

Activities >
Each lesson consists of a structured activity, a communicative activity, and a task based activity. All units include a "Bonus activity" that can add to the lesson.

Discussion Questions >
Each lesson has a short series of discussion questions that relate to the topic and encourage the use of asking follow up questions.

Boxes >
Several boxes are found throughout the text and have different functions

- **Recycle Box**
Reminds the student of language points they have used previously in SLE.

- **Third Wheel**
Gives a suggestion of how students can perform an activity with an extra student.

- **Do You Know?**
Explains the reason why language is used in a specific way.

- **Do You Remember?**
Reminds students of vocabulary from a previous lesson.

- **Tip**
Gives a tip on how the student can acquire the language easier.

Segue Activity >
The segue activity consists of a reading that relates to the topic of the listening, discussion questions which check the comprehension of the reading, and a short writing task on the topic.

Goals for the Course:

1
You should be able to use the following grammatical structures:

a Using "it" as the subject

b The simple past vs. The present perfect

c Expressing consequence with the zero conditional

d Participle adjectives

e Prepositions of location

f Using "there is" and "there are"

g Degrees of certainty

h Expressing preference with "would rather"

i Lengths of time with the simple past and present perfect

2
You should be able to perform the following functions:

a Asking for permission and favors

b Describing where things are made and what they are made of

c Giving warnings and showing prohibition

d Expressing Prohibition and Necessity

e Making exceptions

f Giving impressions

g Giving directions

h Reporting questions

i Expressing similarities and differences

- Making recommendations and suggestions
- Giving advice
- Comparisons

Did You Know?
"Get in" vs. "Get on"

These two phrasal verbs are very similar! When talking about travel, "get on" is generally used for vehicles in which you can stand, and "get in" is used for vehicles in which you must sit.

3rd wheel
If you are the third member in this activity, interrupt the speakers politely, offer your own greeting, and join the conversation.

Tip What's a follow-up question? Asking a follow-up question is an important part of keeping a conversation going. By asking follow-up questions you are showing interest in the conversation.

objectives:
- Use indirect questions
- Listen to a story about scams

Do You Remember?
creativity
patience
dedication
honesty
social skills
organization
judgment
passion

• see glossary for definitions

Need to Know:

• **to be fired**
Lucas **was fired** from his job because he stole money from the safe.

• **to be laid off**
Because of budget cuts, thirty employees **were laid off** last week.

• **to retire**
My parents **retired** when they were 60 years old.

• **to quit**
She **quit** her job because the salary was too low.

• **to get promoted**
When Fred **got promoted**, he received a higher salary.

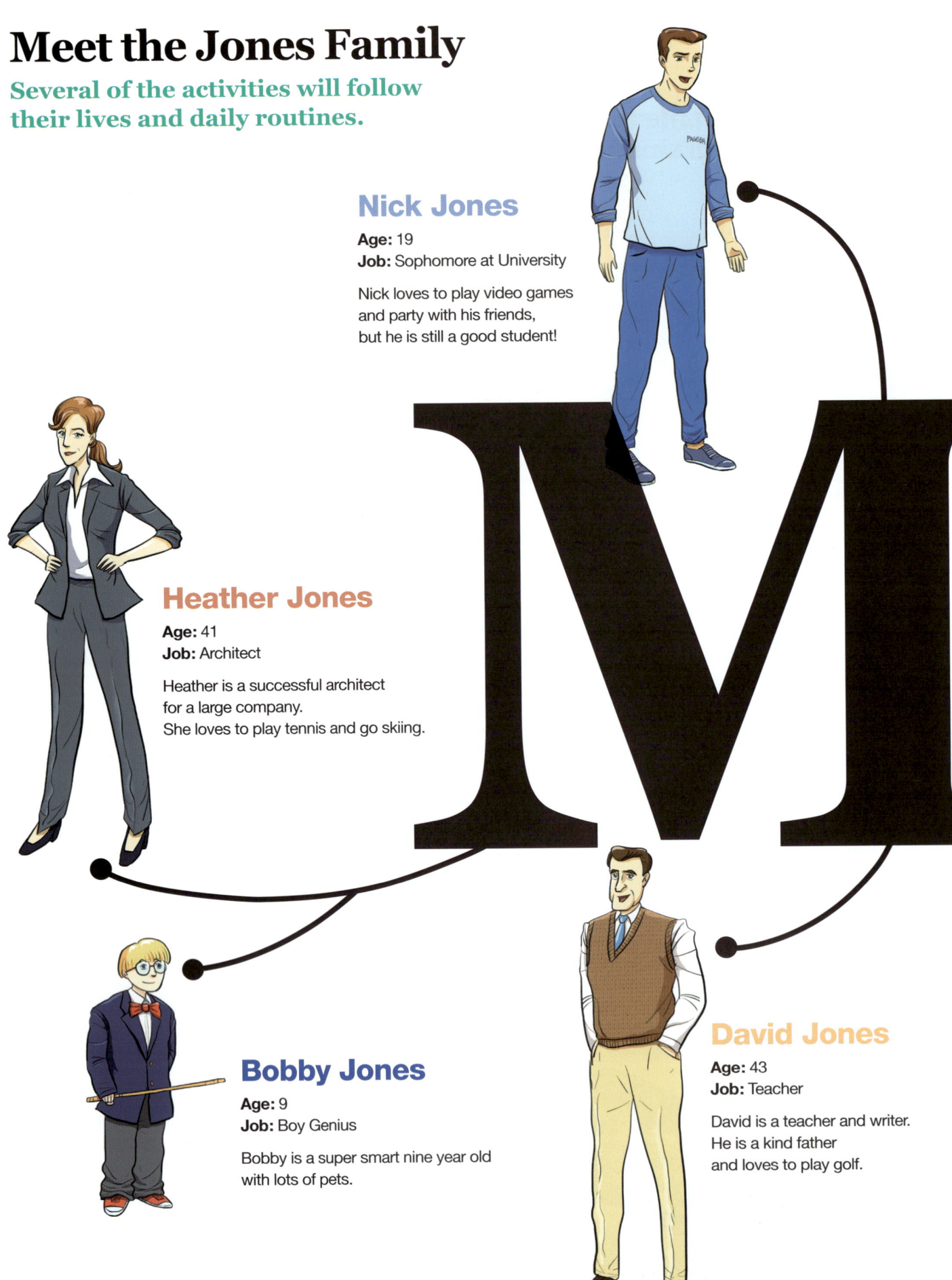

01
Been There, Done That
Introductions & Experiences

Objectives:
/ Discussing how to acquire language
/ Using "it" to refer to the subject

WARM UP

PART 1

1. Do you think English is easy or hard to learn? Why?
   - What is the most difficult part of English for you?
     -Reading
     -Writing
     -Speaking
     -Listening

PART 2

1. What is something you would like to learn? (besides English)
   - Where is the best place to learn this:
     -self study?
     -with friends?
     -in a class?

2. What is something (besides English) that took you a long time to learn?
   - How did you learn this? (practice, instruction, watching others, etc.)

LESSON 1

A. Things Take Time

PART 1 ● With a partner, discuss the questions. Give reasons for your opinions.

1. **How long does it take to become fluent in English?**

   I think it takes _____ because…

Nine months | Nine years | Other

The time needed to learn a language is different for everyone. Even native speakers are still learning.

2. **How are these things similar to learning English?**

   _____ is like learning English because…

Learning an instrument | Learning how to paint | Learning chemistry

Every skill is gained by practicing. Some things might be easier for you and much harder for others.

3. **Which of these is it important to study if you want to become a better English speaker?**

   It is important to study _____ because…

Reading | Vocabulary / Grammar | Writing

All skills lead to better speaking, but study must also include speaking practice.

Fluent (*adj.*): able to communicate like a native

PART 2

> Choose one set of questions (A, B, C, D).
> Make questions using one choice.
> Remember some of your partner's answers to your questions, so you can tell the class about them.

Tip The language used in these questions is covered in 1B. Is there anything you need to review?

A

1. What does _____ mean?
   a. your name
   b. the word "fluent"
   c. (other)

2. What do you think about _____?
   a. bungee jumping
   b. horror movies
   c. (other)

3. What could I do _____?
   a. this weekend
   b. for a unique vacation
   c. (other)

B

1. Whose smart phone is _____?
   a. bigger
   b. more expensive
   c. (other)

2. What is close to your _____?
   a. home
   b. office/school
   c. (other)

3. How often do you _____?
   a. see your friends from high school
   b. exercise
   c. (other)

C

1. Do you prefer _____ or _____?
   a. Asian food or Western food
   b. summer or winter
   c. (other)

2. What do you do when you are _____?
   a. bored
   b. tired
   c. (other)

3. What do you have to do _____?
   a. every day
   b. this month
   c. (other)

D

1. What makes you _____?
   a. laugh
   b. angry
   c. (other)

2. What's wrong / right with _____?
   a. your neighborhood
   b. your city
   c. (other)

3. What were you doing _____?
   a. when you met your best friend
   b. while you were at home last night
   c. (other)

PART 3
When your instructor asks you what your partner said, respond by telling the class something you learned.
_____ said he/she _____.

Example:
Jenny said she prefers eating fast food more than her mom's food.

Unit 1 Been There, Done That | 13

B. It's Not Easy Being Green

Language Point: Using "it" as the subject

It is often used to refer to time or weather.

A: *How long does it take? What's it like outside?*
B: *It takes about an hour. It's snowing pretty hard.*

It can also refer to something that comes later in the sentence.
▸ *It takes a long time to learn a new language.*
Learning a new language is the subject.

Tip A common mistake is to say:
I am hard to learn English.
Replace *I am* with *It is.*
It is hard to learn English.

Pre-listening

1. Sports: Are these sports hard or easy to learn?
   • Which is the hardest to learn?

   Example: Work out
   *It's easy to learn how to **work out**, but it takes a long time to get results.*

Sports:

 billiards   basketball   volleyball  soccer (football)

 baseball   tennis  table tennis   football

bowling golf  working out   badminton

motor sports archery   diving   climbing

Work out (*phrasal v.*): exercise

2. School Subjects: Are these subjects hard or easy to learn?
   • Which one takes the most time?

Listening  TRACK 2-3

Grandpa is learning how to do something new.
Listen, and check the box next to the thing he is actually learning.

Coding (*n.*): writing computer programs

Unit 1 Been There, Done That | 15

Post-listening

How many months or years do you think it takes to become an expert in the following things? What skills does it take to become an expert? Take turns asking your partner.

Example: Cook like a pro

A: *How long does it take to cook like a pro?*
B: *I think it takes about five years to learn how to cook like a pro.*
A: *What skills does it take to learn to cook like a pro?*
B: *It takes plenty of practice and training with other skilled cooks.*

Years

1. remember people's names

2. drive a car

3. write Chinese characters

4. earn a black belt

5. learn a musical instrument

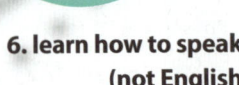
6. learn how to speak _____ (not English)

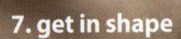
7. get in shape

> Which of the above things can you do?
> What was the hardest part about learning it?
> What was the easiest part?

C. The Maven

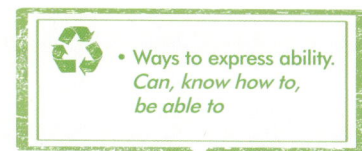
- Ways to express ability. Can, know how to, be able to

PART 1

How skilled are you at life?

> Ask your partner which of the life skills he/she has. Ask a follow-up question.
> Check the boxes, and add up your score at the bottom.

> **Example: Count to ten in Chinese**
> **A:** *Can you count to ten in Chinese?*
> **B:** *Sure.*
> **A:** *Can you prove it?*

1. draw an animal ◯
2. take a good photo ◯
3. **twirl** a pen in your fingers ◯
4. drive a car ◯
5. change a **diaper** ◯
6. **iron** a shirt ◯
7. swim across a pool ◯
8. dance like a robot ◯
9. make a paper airplane ◯
10. **sew** a button ◯
11. give directions to your house ◯
12. do ten **push ups** ◯
13. do a load of laundry ◯
14. make a **spreadsheet** ◯
15. tie a necktie ◯

Maven (*n.*): an expert
Twirl (*v.*): turn, spin
Diaper (*n.*): piece of cloth or plastic, worn on the bottom by babies
Iron (*v.*): press a hot piece of metal on cloth to make it smooth
Sew (*v.*): use a needle and thread to make or fix clothing
Pushup (*n.*): exercise pushing the body up from the floor with the arms
Spreadsheet (*n.*): document with information in rows and columns; calculates numbers

do you have THE SKILLS?

These are worth 2 points.

16. make a cocktail ◯
17. change a tire ◯
18. give a **compliment** ◯
19. hold a **newborn** baby ◯
20. solve: (√2 - √3)² =* ◯
21. climb a mountain ◯
22. catch a fish ◯
23. make a phone app ◯
24. say please and thank you in three languages ◯
25. remember people's names ◯
26. cook pancakes ◯
27. sing the **national anthem** ◯
28. tell a joke ◯
29. perform **CPR** ◯
30. read music ◯

*the square root of two minus the square root of three, quantity squared

POINTS

35-45: Most interesting person in the room.
25-34: Truly skilled.
15-24: Well-rounded person.
5-14 : On your way. Keep learning.
0-4 : Time to study, buddy!

PART 2 • Think of another skill you have. Ask your classmates if they are able to do it.

Compliment (*n.*): positive comment
Newborn (*adj.*): baby that has recently been born
National anthem (*n.*): official song of a country
CPR (Cardio Pulmonary Respiration) (*n.*): emergency treatment for stopped heartbeat

Discussion Questions

1. How long does it take you to...
   - get dressed and ready to leave the house in the morning?
   - get from home to work (or school)?
   - eat lunch?
   - fall asleep after going to bed?

2. How long did it take you to...
   - learn to read well?
   - finish university?
   - learn to do your job?

3. Is it easy or hard for you to...
   - talk to strangers?
   - **memorize** new words?
   - wake up in the morning?
   - find a place without a map?

4. Is it easier for you to understand spoken English or read in English? Why?

5. Is it harder for you to speak English with native speakers or with non-native speakers? Why?

6. What do you like most about English?
   - What do you dislike most about English?

Memorize *(v.)*: to remember something

LESSON 2

>> WARM UP

Objectives:
/ Comparing the past
/ Talking about experiences

**Which of the following experiences are important to you?
Which one is the most important to you?**

Getting your first car
Graduating
Getting your first award
Getting married
Starting your first job
Having a baby
Experiences

**Which of these experiences did you have in the past?
Which of the experiences do you want to have in the future?**

A. The Past Is In The Past

Language Point : The Present Perfect vs. The Simple Past

The present perfect: *Have/Has* + past participle

> The *present perfect* is used to talk about something that happened before now. The exact time is unimportant.
> ▸ *Has Daniel been to Spain?*
>   *Yes, he has. -Or- No, he hasn't.*
>
> The *simple past* is used when there is a specific mention of time.
> ▸ *Daniel went to Spain last July.*

PART 1 • Answer the questions using the present perfect.
If there is a specific time, say when it was using the simple past.

Ali

Marital status: single, never married
Major: undecided
Languages: English, Arabic, French
Hobbies: soccer, sailing
Favorite city: Rio de Janeiro
Happiest memory: getting accepted to university

1994: Born in Dubai
2002: Moved to Toronto
2010: Soccer team won regional championship
2012: Started university in Montreal
2013: Traveled to Brazil
2014: Started tennis lessons

1. Has Ali visited South America?
2. Has he studied mathematics?
3. Has he learned Korean?
4. What sports has Ali tried?
5. Has Ali ever been on a boat?
6. Has he chosen a major?
7. Has he lived in the Middle East?
8. Has he ever settled down?

Settle down (*phrasal v.*): get married and start a family

PART 2 ● Ask your partner what he/she has done in the past year. After he/she answers, ask a follow-up question.

Example: been / doctor

Have you *been* to the *doctor* this year?

A: Yes, I have.
B: *When did you go?*
-Or-
A: No, I haven't.
B: *When was the last time you went?*

1. eat / Italian

2. buy / shoes

3. have / a cold

4. go / a trip

5. see / a movie

6. watch / sunrise

7. changed / phones

8. lose / something

B. Never Have I Ever

Language Point : Asking Questions about Experience

It is common to add the word *ever* to the present perfect to find out about having an experience at any time in the past.
▸ *Have you ever seen a comet?*
Answering-
+ *Yes, I have. / Yes, I've seen a comet.*
- *No, I haven't. / No, I've never seen a comet.*

Incorrect: *Yes, I have ever seen a comet.*

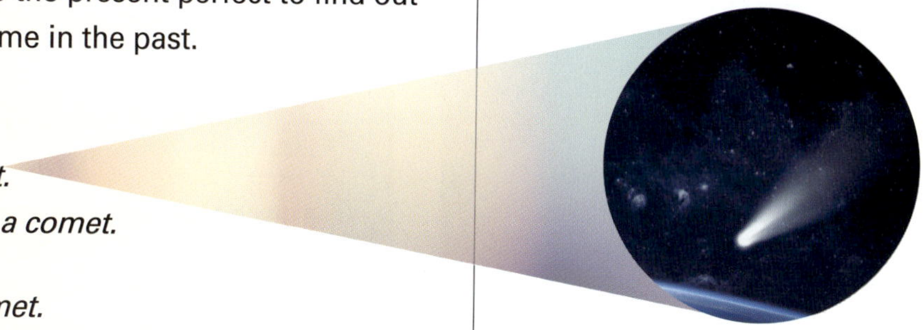

PART 1 ● Make questions using the pictures and the verbs. Use the present perfect to ask about experience.

Have you ever...?

- an **accordion** / a truck / a **durian** / dolphins
- **heard / ridden / driven** — a horse
- **smelled / seen / visited** — India
- **drunk / cooked / flown in** — bubble tea / a holiday dinner / a helicopter
- **done / made / eaten** — yoga / natto / a snowman

Yes, I have. / No, I haven't.

Accordion (*n.*): a musical instrument with a keyboard and buttons
Durian (*n.*): fruit from South East Asia
Natto (*n.*): Japanese fermented soybeans

PART 2 ● Now, use the simple past to get more details.

> **Example: Drive a truck**
> **A:** *When did you last drive a truck?*
> **B:** *I last drove a truck just yesterday. I drive one for my job!*

1. When did you drive…?
I drove…

2. When did you fly in…?
I flew in…

3. When did you smell…
I smelled…

4. When did you hear…?
I heard…

5. When did you see…?
I saw…

6. When did you visit…?
I visited…

7. When did you do…?
I did…

8. When did you ride…?
I rode…

9. When did you drink…?
I drank…

10. When did you make…?
I made…

11. When did you cook…?
I cooked…

12. When did you eat…?
I ate…

Now, think of a few other "have you ever" questions to ask your partners.
Have you ever…

C. Before I Kick the Bucket

> **Bucket List:** a list of things that someone has to do sometime in their life

PART 1

> Ask your partner(s) if he/she has done the things on the list.
> Answer with: **Yes, I have.** (Say what happened.)
> **No, I haven't, but I want to.** (Say why you want to.)
> -Or- **No, I haven't, and I don't want to.** (Say why you don't want to.)

Example: Plant a tree and watch it grow

A: *Have you ever planted a tree and watched it grow?*
B: *No, I haven't, but I want to. It sounds like a really positive thing to do.*

A. Travel List

Have you ever...

1.
visited Machu Picchu?
- ☐ Yes, I have.
- ☐ No, I haven't, but I want to.
- ☐ No, I haven't, and I don't want to.

2.
lived in a different country?
- ☐ Yes, I have.
- ☐ No, I haven't, but I want to.
- ☐ No, I haven't, and I don't want to.

3.
attended **Carnival** or the World Cup?
- ☐ Yes, I have.
- ☐ No, I haven't, but I want to.
- ☐ No, I haven't, and I don't want to.

4.
gone on a **safari**?
- ☐ Yes, I have.
- ☐ No, I haven't, but I want to.
- ☐ No, I haven't, and I don't want to.

5.
visited...(_____)?
- ☐ Yes, I have.
- ☐ No, I haven't, but I want to.
- ☐ No, I haven't, and I don't want to.

Add two questions of your own.
1. Have you ever...
2. Have you ever...
Do you want to add any of your partner's ideas to your list?

Carnival (*n.*): public festival celebrated before Lent; famous in Brazil
Safari (*n.*): a trip to see animals

B. Experience List

Have you ever...

1 learned how to surf?
- ☐ Yes, I have.
- ☐ No, I haven't, but I want to.
- ☐ No, I haven't, and I don't want to.

2 ridden a (horse, camel, elephant)?
- ☐ Yes, I have.
- ☐ No, I haven't, but I want to.
- ☐ No, I haven't, and I don't want to.

3 done something extreme?
- ☐ Yes, I have.
- ☐ No, I haven't, but I want to.
- ☐ No, I haven't, and I don't want to.

4 climbed a mountain?
- ☐ Yes, I have.
- ☐ No, I haven't, but...
- ☐ No, I haven't, and...

5 flown an airplane?
- ☐ Yes, I have.
- ☐ No, I haven't, but...
- ☐ No, I haven't, and...

Add 2 questions of your own.
1. Have you ever...
2. Have you ever...
Do you want to add any of your partner's ideas to your list?

C. Lifestyle / Career List

Have you ever...

1 quit a job you hated?
- ☐ Yes, I have.
- ☐ No, I haven't, but...
- ☐ No, I haven't, and...

2 started your own business?
- ☐ Yes, I have.
- ☐ No, I haven't, but...
- ☐ No, I haven't, and...

3 written a book?
- ☐ Yes, I have.
- ☐ No, I haven't, but...
- ☐ No, I haven't, and...

4 sung in front of an audience?
- ☐ Yes, I have.
- ☐ No, I haven't, but...
- ☐ No, I haven't, and...

5 bought a (car, house, etc.)?
- ☐ Yes, I have.
- ☐ No, I haven't, but...
- ☐ No, I haven't, and...

Add 2 questions of your own.
1. Have you ever...
2. Have you ever...
Do you want to add any of your partner's ideas to your list?

PART 2
What things from above would you put on your bucket list? *I would...*

Discussion Questions

1 Have you been abroad?
   - When did you first go abroad? Where did you go?
   - When did you last travel overseas?
   - What is the most interesting country you have visited?

2 Have you ever met a famous person?
   - Who was it?
   - Where and when did you meet?

3 Have you ever forgotten a person's name? What happened?
   - When did you last forget a person's name?
   - Have you ever gotten angry because somebody forgot your name?

4 What is one food you have never eaten but want to?
   - Why do you want to eat this food?
   - How about a food you have never eaten and don't want to?

5 What is something you have tried to learn but failed?
   - What made it so difficult?
   - Would you try to learn it again?

UNIT 1 REVIEW

How well can you use…
- ☐ Expressions for asking about additional information?
- ☐ Ways to report what other people have said?

What do you need to study more?

Activity: The Best of the Best

Ask your classmates about the best things that have happened to them.

Example: The best movie I have seen

A: *What's the best movie you have ever seen?*
B: *The best movie I have ever seen is Dracula. I started staying awake all night and sleeping all day after I saw it!*

- The best movie I have seen
- The funniest joke I have heard
- The most delicious food I have eaten
- The most interesting book I have read
- The most beautiful music I have heard
- The best vacation I have taken
- The scariest thing I have experienced
- The most boring TV program I have watched
- The spiciest thing I have tasted
- The dirtiest room I have slept in
- (other)

Segue

A. Discussion
1. Have you ever taken a class to learn something? (other than an English class)
   - What did you learn?
2. What types of continuing education classes would you like to try?
   - Why would you like to learn that?

B. Writing
Imagine you were going to teach a class on something you are good at. Write a paragraph describing the course, how long the students will need to study, and how much it will cost.

02
Tailor Made
Politeness & Description

Objectives:
/ Review location language
/ Practice asking for permission and favors

WARM UP

PART 1

What are the last three things you bought?
1.
2.
3.

-Where did you buy them?
-Did you get a good deal?

PART 2

1. Did you go shopping with someone the last time you shopped?
2. Do you like shopping with someone or shopping alone?
3. How often do you go shopping?

TONGUE TWISTERS

- Preshrunk silk shirts.

LESSON 1

A. Mall Rats

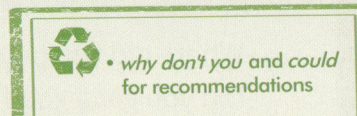 • *why don't you* and *could* for recommendations

Language Point : Describing Location in a Building

On a floor of a building
▸ *He lives on the second floor.*

Above another floor
▸ *He lives above a convenience store.*

Under another floor
▸ *There is parking under the mall.*

In front of a room or store
▸ *I'm waiting in front of the computer store.*

In/Inside a room or store
▸ *She's in the bathroom.*

Next to another room or store
▸ *It's next to the bedroom.*

1 shoelaces
2 some magazines
3 some records
4 vitamins
5 a stuffed animal
6 french fries
7 a scarf
8 a gold chain
9 a SIM card
10 office supplies
11 some candles
12 a melon

PART 1
> You are looking for several items at the mall on the next page, and you're not sure where to buy them.
> Ask your partner for a suggestion.

Example: A coffee

A: Where can I buy a cup of coffee?
B: Why don't you go to Queequeg Coffee?
A: Where's that?
B: It's on the first floor in front of Fearless Fashion.

ALBEE SQUARE MALL

PART 2

> What is your favorite shopping area?
> What do you like to buy there?
> Where in your favorite shopping area can I find that item?

B. Give and Take

Language Point : Asking for Permission

There are many ways to sound polite. Some sound more formal than others.

Polite — **Very Polite**

Can I...?
Can I get a dozen?

Could I...?
Could I have a dozen?

May I please...?
May I please have a dozen?

Pre-listening

Take turns asking for permission. Ask your partner why he/she needs it.
Then, give an answer based on how polite you think they are.

Example: stay at your house

A: *Can I stay at your house tonight?*
B: *Why?*
A: *Because I'm too lazy to take the bus home.*
B: *Uh. No way!*

1. use your car?
2. use your phone?
3. stay at your house?
4. take your picture?
5. change the TV channel?
6. borrow some money?
7. copy your notes from last class?
8. borrow your _____?

Listening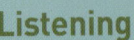

Nick just got a part-time job in a café at the mall.
His mom stops by to get a cup of coffee.
Write the three prices Jack gives for coffee in the boxes.

Post-listening

Language Point: Asking for Favors

Tip: Don't use *May* when asking for favors.
Incorrect: *May you help me tie my shoe?*

Polite ←→ Very Polite

Asking:	Can you...?	Could you...?	Would you please...?
Answering:	Sure.	Certainly.	I'd be happy to.

> Take turns asking your partner for favors.
> You must answer yes, and then ask the follow-up questions.
> You can also ask, *"What will you do for me?"*

1. help me move
- What day are you moving?
- Where are you moving to?
- How long will it take?

2. take me to the airport
- What day do you have to go?
- When does your plane leave?
- What airline are you flying?

3. make me a cup of coffee
- Do you want sugar or milk?
- Do you prefer strong or weak coffee?
- Would you like it hot or iced?

4. pick up my clothes at the dry cleaner
- How many pieces are there?
- How much will it cost?
- What time does the dry cleaner close?

5. lend me some money
- How much do you need?
- Why do you need it?
- When can you pay me back?

6. help me with my homework
- What are you studying?
- Where do you want to study?
- How long do I need to help you?

7. teach me how to dance
- What kind of dancing?
- Where do you want to practice?
- When do you want to start?

8. find a blind date for me
- How old should he/she be?
- What should he/she look like?
- How tall should he/she be?

C. Shopping Spree Challenge

You won a shopping spree at Big Easy Department Store. Here are the rules:
> You have $3000 to spend. You must buy something in every department you choose to enter.
> You can only visit one department on each floor.
> Take turns being the shopper and the clerks of the different departments.

Start by practicing the conversation on the first floor.

BIG EASY DEPARTMENT STORE

1st Floor (choose one)

Clerk: *May I help you?*
Shopper: *Could you show me your phones?*
C: *Certainly. We have the:*

S: *What's the difference?*
C: *The Fuss Free 1000 is _____.*
      The I-Universe is _____.
S: *Could I have the _____?*
C: *Yes, certainly.*

$50

Fuss Free 1000
inexpensive
easy to use

$300

The I-Universe III-X
high quality
powerful

Cell Phone Department

Do you want to go to the shoe, the camera, or the jacket department next?

Shopping spree (*n.*): a short period of spending a lot of money

2nd Floor (choose one)

Shoe Department

C: *Hello. How can I help you?*

 $50 — **K-Kasuals** trendy, casual

 $100 — **Super Fits** light, comfortable

Camera Department

C: *What can I do for you?*

 $100 — **Insta-roid** cute, easy

 $400 — **D-Super** expensive, professional

Jacket Department

C: *Good day. May I help you?*

 $150 — **Slik Leather** stylish, durable

 $100 — **Hikers Island** warm, easy to clean

3rd Floor (choose one)

Sunglasses Department

 $100 — **Rode blocks** scratch resistant, sporty

 $50 — **Wray-bandz** light, fashionable

Watch Department

 $200 — **I Time** digital, techie

 $300 — **Brolex** analog, classic

Electronics Department

$1500 — **Magnetbox** huge, crystal clear

$1000 — **Probook** portable, well designed

Durable (*adj.*): strong; hard to break
Resistant (*adj.*): not easily damaged by something
Portable (*adj.*): easy to carry

Unit 2 Tailor Made | 37

4th Floor (choose one)

Gourmet Department

$25
Choco Fantasy
rich
delicious

$75
Big Red Wine
flavorful
vintage

Cosmetics Department

$100
Smac
natural
glamorous

$75
Mist-ique
unisex
fragrant

Travel Department

comfortable
not crowded
Bud's Bus Tours — **$200**

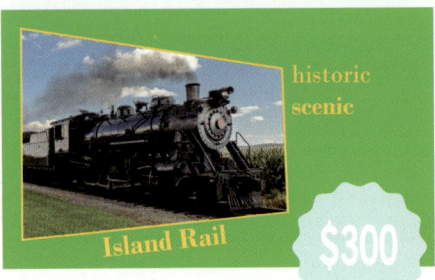

historic
scenic
Island Rail — **$300**

5th Floor (choose one)

$250
Express-o
fast
convenient

$150
Juicer
natural
refreshing

Appliance Department

$500
Snow Bird
quick
durable

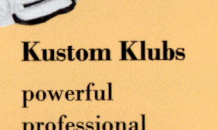

$750
Kustom Klubs
powerful
professional

Sports Department

$1000
Biggo Sofa
soft
comfortable

Massage Chair
relaxing
soothing
$750

Furniture Department

Finish

Add up your total: _____

> The person who is the closest to the $3000 limit without going over is the winner!

Glamorous (*adj.*): stylish and beautiful
Unisex (*adj.*): used by both males and females
Scenic (*adj.*): having a pretty view
Soothing (*adj.*): able to make calm

Discussion Questions

1. How often do you go shopping?
   - ▶ Do you prefer to stay home and shop online or go to a mall and shop? Why?

2. Is it better to shop in a big department store or go to many different small stores?
   - ▶ What is the difference?

3. In what stores can you ask for a discount?
   - ▶ How often do you do this?

4. Do men and women have different shopping habits?
   - ▶ If you think yes, how are their habits different?
   - ▶ If you think no, how are they similar?

5. Do you ask for help from staff in stores? Why or why not?

6. How would you spend $100 if someone gave it to you?
   - ▶ How about $1000?

7. Is it better to buy designer brands that cost more or to buy cheaper brands and save money?
   - ▶ What are the advantages of buying one over the other?

LESSON 2

>> WARM UP

Objectives:
/ Discuss where things are made
/ Discuss what things are made of

In your opinion, which company makes the best…

phone? car? perfume / cologne?

Now, compare each of the items you chose with the items your classmates chose.

> How are these items similar?
> How are they different?
> What is more important to you in the above products: good quality, good design, or brand recognition?

A. Made Men

Language Point: Describing Where Something is Made

made + in: to describe the location
▸ *My watch was made in China. What a surprise.*

made + by: to describe the person or company
▸ *My watch is made by Watchco.*

Tip: *"Made by hand"* and *"hand-made"* have the same meaning: the item is made by a person rather than a machine.

PART 1

A. Take turns asking a partner about the things they own using *Where* and *Who*.

Example: Phone
A: *Who made your phone?*
B: *My phone was made by Acme Phone Company.*
A: *Where was your phone made?*
B: *My phone was made here in this country!*

1. Phone
2. Bag / Purse
3. Shoes
4. Jacket
5. Pen / Pencil
6. Glasses
7. Favorite snack
8. Book
9. TV
10. Computer

B. Think of something else your classmates might like. Ask them...

Who makes your favorite _____?

Language Point: Describing the Materials

Made + of: to describe material
▸ *My shoes are made of leather, and his shoes are made of canvas.*

PART 2 • STUDENT A

- Think of an item that is made of one or more of the materials at the bottom. Don't tell your partner(s).
- Answer the questions about material with:
  yes, no, or *partly.*
- Answer the other questions and give clues if it's really difficult.

STUDENT B

Ask yes/no questions to find out what your partner is thinking of.

- Start with questions about what the item is made of. *(Is it made of metal?)*
- Also, ask questions about the item's purpose or maker. *(Is it used for sending messages?)*
- Make a guess about the item, or ask for **clues** if you need help. *(Is it a cell phone?)*

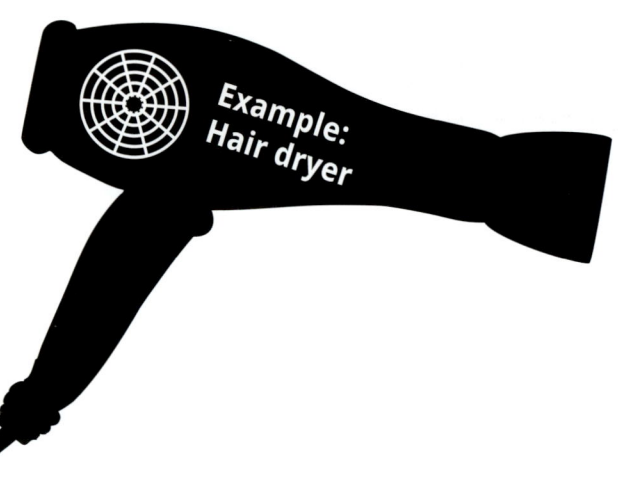

Example: Hair dryer

B: *Is this thing made of plastic?*
A: *Partly, and also metal.*
B: *Is it used inside the house?*
A: *Yes, it is. Usually, after showering.*
B: *Okay. Is it an electric toothbrush?*
A: *No, it isn't.*

Do You Remember?

- "Used for + ing" and "Used to" describe purpose.
A hair dryer is used to dry hair.

Metal   Cloth   Plastic   Wood   Rubber   Paper/Cardboard   Glass   Leather   Stone

MATERIALS

Clue (*n.*): helpful information

B. The Old and The New

For each pair, compare the old-fashioned version to the modern version.

A. How is the old one different from the new one? (What is it made of?, Who is it made by?, etc.)

B. What was good about the old ones? What is better about the new ones?

> **Example: Airplanes**
> **A:** *How are old airplanes different from new ones?*
> **B:** *Old airplanes were made of cloth and wood, but now airplanes are made of steel and plastic.*
> **C:** *The first airplanes were made by inventors like the Wright brothers, but now they are made by big companies like Airbus.*
> **A:** *What was good about the old ones? What's better about the new ones?*

 Sail ships | Cruise ships

 **Rotary** phones | Smartphones

 Coins | Credit cards / Cash

Handmade clothes | Machine-made clothes

 Traditional houses | Modern buildings

What other things have changed a lot?

Rotary (*adj.*): turning

Unit 2 Tailor Made | 43

C. Kimchi Tacos

PART 1 ● Your job is to create **fusion** products and services from the cultures of different places. With a partner, brainstorm some fusion food products from the places below or from some additional places that you can think of.

Korea
Food and drinks: kimchi, rice cakes, Choco pies, soju

Hawaii U.S.A.
Food and drinks: Hawaiian barbecue, spam sushi, blue Hawaii (cocktail)

Mexico
Food and drinks: tacos, ceviche (raw fish in lime juice), mole (spicy chocolate sauce), margaritas

India
Food and drinks: curry, chutney, flatbreads, mango lassi

Thailand
Food and drinks: green curry, Thai noodles, Thai iced tea

Angola
Food and drinks: goat stew, fried **caterpillars**, palm wine (liquor from palm trees)

Example: Korea and India

A: *How about a cocktail made of soju and mango lassi?*
B: *That sounds alright. We can call it mango sossi!*

Fusion (*adj.*): mixing of two or more things
Caterpillar (*n.*): an insect that becomes a butterfly

Discuss various products, interests, and hobbies. Which ones could make good combinations?

> **Example:**
>
> **A:** *Taekwondo and yoga could be a good combination.*
>
> **B:** *Sure. Yoga stretching will make you a better kicker, and Taekwondo will add excitement to the class.*

Hawaii U.S.A.

Interests and Hobbies:
Surfing, Ukulele music

Clothing and Fashion:
Hula skirts and Lei (flower necklaces)

India

Interests and Hobbies:
Yoga, Bollywood movies

Clothing and Fashion:
Saris

Korea

Interests and Hobbies:
Taekwondo, K-pop, Korean hiphop

Clothing and Fashion:
Hanbok

Thailand

Interests and Hobbies:
Muay Thai, Takraw (soccer / volleyball)

Clothing and Fashion:
Pha Nung (Thai dresses)

Mexico

Interests and Hobbies:
Mariachi music, Mexican wrestling

Clothing and Fashion:
Sombreros

Angola

Interests and Hobbies:
Kizomba (Angolan-style Latin dance), Ware (chess-like game)

Clothing and Fashion:
Panos (wraparound garments)

PART 2 ● Now, design several new products, services, and hobbies. Give each new creation a name and explain it to your partner.

> **Example:**
> **A:** *Let's combine Mexican wrestling with traditional Angolan masks to make a new sport: the Masked Warrior Challenge!*
> **B:** *Sounds exciting but a little dangerous!*

Products	A	B	Fusion
Interests:			
Fashion:			
Entertainment:			

With a partner, create a store to sell your items.

- Where will the store be located?
- Who do you think will shop at your store?
- How much will your products and services cost?
- What is the name of your store?

Discussion Questions

1. What are traditional houses in your country made of?
   - ▶ Would you like to live in one? Why or why not?

2. How about the traditional clothing of your country?
   - ▶ What different materials can they be made of?
   - ▶ How are they different from the traditional clothes of other countries?

3. How are clothes made for old people different from clothes made for teenagers and young adults?

4. Would you ever buy a counterfeit designer product? Why or why not?
   - ▶ Is there a big difference in quality between real and **imitation** brand-name products?
   - ▶ Where are the best products made?

5. Would you try a dish made of a poisonous fish?
   - ▶ Would you eat a dish made of an exotic animal? (bear, tiger, etc.)

6. Would you ever wear a necklace made of bones? Why or why not?
   - ▶ Would you ever wear a shirt made of cat hair?
   - ▶ Would you ever wear a hat made of pigeon feathers?
   - ▶ Would you use a toilet made of gold?
   - ▶ Would you use a phone made of leather?

UNIT 2 REVIEW

How well can you use…
- ☐ Ways to ask for permission or favors?
- ☐ Ways to describe where things are made and what they are made of?

What do you need to study more?

Imitation *(adj.)*: copied

Activity: CJ's Logo Shop

Create a new business by following the steps.

1. Choose a logo for your business.

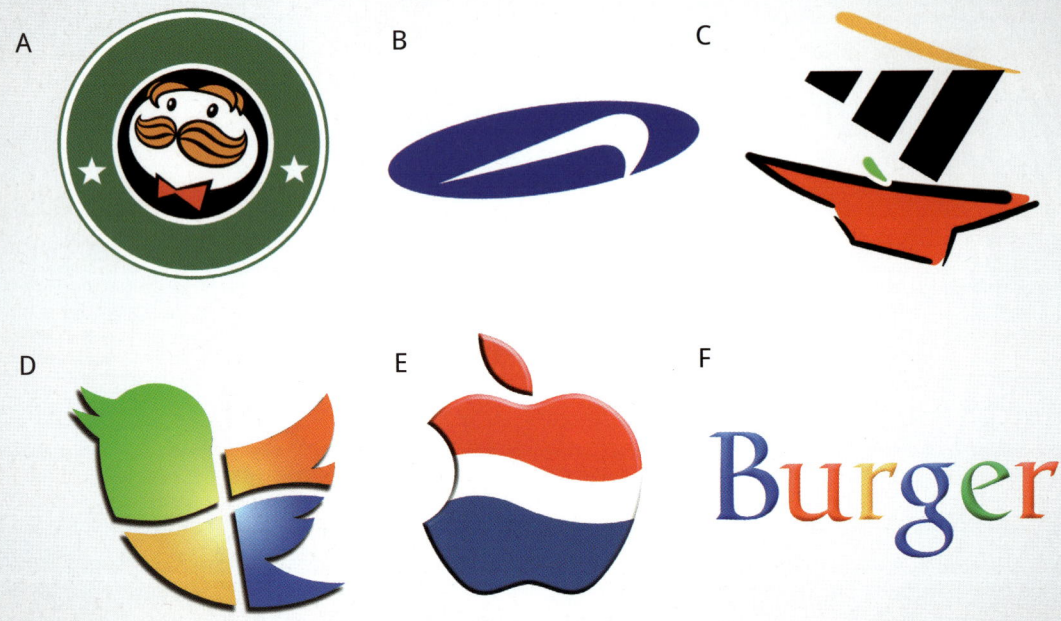

Example:
A: *Our company is called the Pag.*
B: *We sell simple, yet quality, English classes at a good price.*

2. Give your business a name.
3. What product do you make and sell?
4. What is this product made of?
5. Where is the product made?
6. How much will you sell it for?
7. How will you advertise this product?
8. When and where will you release this product?

Customer suggestion and comment page.

Queequeg Coffee
COFFEE & RESTAURANT

LEAVE A COMMENT

MZ92129-
Could you PLEASE tell your baristas not to ask for my name whenever I order coffee. I know the reason is to make your café more "friendly", but my name is Maise. MAY-ZEE not MICE-E. They never get this right. It's really annoying. Could you just call out the name of the coffee you prepared? I mean how many people order decaf half-sweet caramel lattes?

Ben10-
Can I make a suggestion? You really need to bring back the old donuts and pastries. The new "natural" snacks you have decided to sell are probably healthier, but they're not tastier. I know people are worried about their weight these days, but I'm not sure how I'm going to make it through my mornings without my two chocolate donuts and cheese pastry.

Heyther-
Would you mind giving Nick at the Queequeg Coffee in Albee Square Mall a raise? He is doing a great job and gave me fantastic service as well as a little something extra in my coffee. Great job, Nick! Oh, and can you also tell him his Mom says hello?

A. Discussion
1. In your opinion, what store or restaurant gives the best customer service?
   ▶ Why do you think so?
2. Have you ever had bad customer service?
   ▶ What happened?
3. What would you say to someone if they gave you bad service?

B. Writing
Think back to a time when you received either good or bad service, and write a short paragraph like the ones above to the company explaining what your problem was or what they did that made you happy.

03
Look Before You Leap
Safety & Prohibition

Objectives:
/ Talk about prohibition and consequence
/ Listen to a dialogue about rules to stay safe

WARM UP

1. What do you think the people in the pictures should or should not be doing?

2. What will happen if they don't follow your advice?

3. What other dangerous situations do we come across in our daily lives?

LESSON 1

A. Without Warning

Language Point : Giving Warnings and Showing Prohibition

Imperative sentences can be used to give warnings or to say something is not allowed. Imperatives have no stated subject.
▸ *Watch out for falling ice.*
▸ *Don't bite your fingernails.*

◇ Note: The word *please* can be used at the beginning of an imperative to make it sound more polite.

PART 1 • With a partner, match the sentence halves to create common parental warnings.

 Don't accept candy...

 Don't stick a fork...

 Look both ways...

 Wash your hands...

 Put a seat belt on...

 Don't play...

A before crossing the street.

B every time you use the bathroom.

C when you ride in the car.

D with matches.

E from strangers.

F in a toaster.

Prohibition (*n.*): stopping somebody from doing something
Imperative (*adj.*): ordering; making somebody do something

Language Point: Showing Consequences

To warn about bad consequences, use *or* to say what will happen when the imperative is not followed.
- *Wear a helmet, or you'll get injured.*
- *Don't go into the tiger cage, or you will get eaten.*

PART 2 • Choose the consequence that matches the previous warnings.

Example:

Don't accept candy from strangers, or you might get kidnapped!

...or you'll get shocked.

...or you'll get hit by a car.

...or you might get **kidnapped**.

...or you'll burn the house down.

...or you'll spread **germs**.

...or you won't be safe in the car.

PART 3 •

What other things do parents tell their children to... eat? do? wear? share? study? watch? What is the consequence of doing or not doing this?

Consequence (*n.*): bad result of an action
Kidnap (*v.*): take away by force
Germs (*n.*): viruses or bacteria

B. Sign Language

Pre-listening

With a partner, match the imperative to a sign. Discuss with your partner why it is important to do or not do these things. Where can you see each sign?

1. Don't touch the animals.
2. Don't put your hand in the water.
3. Don't drink the water.
4. Keep dogs on a **leash**.
5. Throw away trash.
6. Don't run by the water.
7. Stay two meters away.
8. Don't feed the animals.
9. Watch your children.
10. Don't take photos.
11. Don't smoke.
12. Don't use cell phones.

Listening  TRACK 6-7

Bobby and his Grandpa are going into a Cave. Put a check in the do symbol or the don't symbol depending on what advice Grandpa gives Bobby.

Post-listening

Language Point : If A, (then) B - True conditions

Make sentences about true conditions in the present by adding an *if clause* to an *imperative*.
▶ *If it is cold outside, take a coat.*   – or –   ▶ *Take a coat if it is cold outside.*
This sentence means that if one condition is true *(cold outside)*,
something needs to happen. *(take a coat)*

◇Note: In these sentences, *If* has the same meaning as *When*.
When it is cold outside, take a coat.

What are some things that are important to do in the following situations? What are some things that you should not do?

1. If you clean the house,...

...open all the windows.
...don't fall out of the window!

2. If you visit another country,...

3. If you go out for a night **on the town**,...

4. If you forget an **appointment**,...

5. If you use the internet,...

6. If you exercise,...

7. If you go on a first date,...

8. If you visit an animal park,...

Leash (*n.*): long piece of cloth used to hold a dog by the neck
Clause (*n.*): a group of words with a subject and predicate
On the town (*idiom*): at a city's nightlife locations such as restaurants and bars
Appointment (*n.*): a scheduled meeting at a specific time

C. The Little Dictators

Start your own island nation. What will it be like? Are you going to be a kind leader or a cruel master? Follow these steps:

PART 1 • **Fantasy Island**
Make your island nation! Work with a partner or group. Give reasons for your choices, and come to an agreement.

A. Give your new nation a name.
_____

B. How many people? (choose 1)
Our island will have…

- millions of people
- hundreds of people 
- just a few people 

C. What is the economy based on? (choose 2)
We will make money with…

- food
- technology 
- entertainment 
- science 
- fashion 

D. What kind of environment will your island have? (choose 2)
Our island will have…

- forests
- grasslands 
- deserts 
- mountains 
- rainforests 

Dictator (n.): a ruler with total control of a country's people

PART 2 • The Law is the Law

Now, make some rules about the following things.
Choose one rule, or think of your own for each of the categories.

1. SCHOOL:
If you are a student,

A. study all day.
B. study a little each day.
C. play. Studying is boring.
D. (other)

2. WORK:
If you have a job,

A. work seven days a week.
B. work five days a week.
C. only work weekends.
D. (other)

3. DATING:
When you go on a date,

A. men pay and buy a gift.
B. split the cost.
C. women pay.
D. (other)

4. FAMILY:
If you have a family,

A. come home right after school/work.
B. hang out only on weekends.
C. don't spend time with those people.
D. (other)

5. FRIENDS:
When you meet friends,

A. turn off your phones.
B. don't drink too much alcohol.
C. don't bring boyfriends/girlfriends.
D. (other)

6. SPORTS:
If the national team plays,

A. wear the team colors.
B. play the game on every channel.
C. don't cheer for the home team.
D. (other)

7. FOOD:
If you go out to eat,

A. eat only meat.
B. eat only vegetables and fish.
C. don't pay when you wait too long.
D. (other)

8. CLOTHING:
If you leave the house,

A. put on your left shoe first.
B. wear only jeans.
C. don't wear hats.
D. (other)

9. PETS:
If you have a pet,

A. pick up all poop.
B. keep it inside.
C. don't give it a funny name.
D. (other)

10. HOUSING:
If you live in an apartment,

A. be quiet after 8 p.m.
B. talk to the neighbors.
C. don't make bad smells.
D. (other)

PART 3 • The Punishment Fits the Crime

What happens if someone breaks one of your laws?
Choose a punishment from the list, or think of your own.

> **Example:**
> If you are a student, study all day, or eat a wasabi sandwich.

1. wear a clown suit for the day.
2. eat a wasabi sandwich.
3. clean the sand on the beach.
4. don't sit for eight hours.
5. hold a sign that tells everyone your crime.
6. get a **verbal** warning. Just don't do it again.
7. spend a night in a **haunted** house.
8. walk around the island _____ time(s).
9. don't leave the house for _____ week(s).
10. don't speak for _____ day(s).
11. throw your _____ into the sea.
12. (other)

PART 4 • You need to attract some tourists to your great island! Use the fact sheet to present your island to the other groups in the class.

Welcome to the island nation of (Your country's name)!

What to expect when visiting:
___(Your country's name)___ is a country of ___(environment)___ and ___(environment)___.
Our economy is based on ___(industry)___ and ___(industry)___.
There are ___(number)___ people in ___(your country's name)___.

There are a few important rules visitors need to remember when visiting:
1.
2.
3.
Any questions?
Enjoy your stay!

58 | SLE Generations 1C

Discussion Questions

1. What behaviors or dangers did your parents warn you about most often when you were a child?
   - Did you often get into trouble when you were a child?
   - What were you told in these situations?

2. In your opinion, why do so many children enjoy playing with matches?
   - What other dangerous activities do children enjoy?

3. Why can't you feed the animals when you visit a zoo?
   - Why can't you touch them?
   - Are there places where you can touch and feed animals?

4. What penalty should drivers get if they drive on a crowded sidewalk?
   - What **penalty** should pedestrians get if they sleep in the middle of a crowded street?
   - What penalty should people get for **littering**?
   - What penalty should people get for driving and talking on the phone?

5. What are things you can't do in your country, but people in other countries can do?
   - What are things you can do in your country that people in other countries can't do?

6. What are some things people should definitely not do on a date?
   - What are some things people should definitely do on a date?

7. What is one rule you think should never be broken?

Verbal (*adj.*): with spoken words
Haunted (*adj.*): having ghosts
Penalty (*n.*): an official punishment
Littering (*n.*): throwing trash on the ground

LESSON 2

>> WARM UP

Objectives:
/ Compare prohibition and necessity
/ Discuss making exceptions

Match the name of the disaster to the picture.

> Tornado
> Earthquake
> Heat Wave
> Flood
> Fire
> Hurricane / Typhoon

1. Does your country ever have these disasters?
2. Have you ever been in one of these disasters?
3. What countries are these disasters common in?

A. Disaster Awareness

Language Point : Prohibition vs. Necessity

Tip: Don't have to ≠ Can't
Can't means something is not allowed. *You can't run. It's against the rules.*
Don't have to means it's okay if you do it, but it's also okay if you don't do it. *You don't have to run. Nobody is chasing you.*

Prohibition ←——————————————————→ Necessity

| you can't run | you'd better not run | you'd better run | you have to run |
| (there is no choice) | (or something bad will happen) | (or something bad will happen) | (there is no choice) |

In each box, choose the right words to make good advice, and explain the reasons.

FIRE
You (had better not/don't have to) ignore the fire and stay in bed.
Why?_____

You (have to/can't) get out of the house immediately.
Why?_____

FLOOD
You (had better/can't) go to higher ground.
Why?_____

You (can't/don't have to) stay in your basement.
Why?_____

HURRICANE / TYPHOON

You (had better/don't have to) leave before the storm arrives.
Why?_____

You (can't/don't have to) take your guitar with you.
Why?_____

HEAT WAVE

Everybody (has to/can't) drink plenty of water, especially older people.
Why?_____

You (can't/have to) leave children or pets in a parked car, even for a few minutes.
Why?_____

TORNADO

You (had better not/don't have to) stay on your roof.
Why?_____

You (don't have to/have to) go to the basement or low ground.
Why?_____

EARTHQUAKE

You (had better/don't have to) cover your head and stay away from glass windows.
Why?_____

You (don't have to/can't) use the elevator.
Why?_____

B. Nobody Wants Problems!

Mr. and Mrs. Smart moved into a new house. Match the pictures with the things they had better or had better not do to keep their house safe. What can happen if they don't do these things?

> **Example: Slippery item on the floor**
> **A:** *What is happening in this picture?*
> **B:** *They'd better not leave **slippery** items on the floor. Someone is going to slip and get hurt.*

- Put knives away
- Buy fire extinguishers
- Put too many cords in an outlet
- Turn off the stove
- Be careful lifting heavy objects
- Install **smoke detectors**
- Leave meat and milk out
- Clean up accidents
- Lock doors
- Leave pills out

What other things do people need to do to stay safe?

What other things should people do to avoid accidents?

Slippery (adj.): easy to slide on a surface
Smoke detector (n.): a device that sets off an alarm when it is aware of smoke

C. Exceptions to The Rule

Language Point : Making Exceptions

The word *unless* can be used in sentences to make an exception.
▶ You can't go in there unless you have permission.

◇Note: *unless* has the same meaning as *if...not*
If you don't have permission, you can't go in there.

Discuss how important the following things are and when to make an exception.

Example: Steal from others
A: *You can't steal from others.*
B: *Well, you can't steal from others unless you're starving.*
A: *Good point.*

1 can't / steal from others

2 have to / follow the speed limit

3 have to / brush your teeth

4 have to / get an education

5 have to / get out in nature

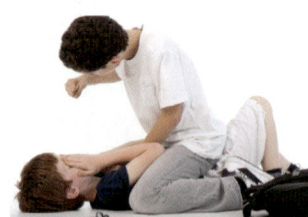
6 can't / fight

7 can't / **gamble**

8 have to / sleep

9 don't have to / get dressed up

10 **swear**

11 say "please" and "thank you"

12 turn off your cell phone

13 exercise

Are there any other dos and don'ts you can think of? Ask your partner about exceptions to these rules.

Gamble (*v.*): playing games with the chance of losing or winning money
Swear (*v.*): say bad words

Discussion Questions

1 What types of natural disasters are you most afraid of? Why?

2 What are some things all people should do to prepare for natural disasters?

3 Some people like to chase tornadoes and other dangerous storms for excitement.
   ▶ What do you think of this?
   ▶ Would you like to try it? Why or why not?

4 What things do you do to stay safe…
   ▶ at home?
   ▶ while driving?
   ▶ when swimming?
   ▶ while drinking?
   ▶ when walking home at night?

5 What are the most common accidents at home?

6 What are some really dangerous jobs?
   ▶ Do you think you could do these jobs? Why or why not?

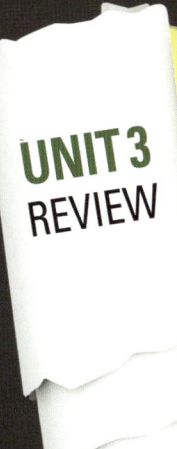

UNIT 3 REVIEW

How well can you use…
☐ Ways to express prohibition and warning?
☐ Expressing exceptions with unless?
What do you need to study more?

Unit 3 Look Before You Leap | 65

Activity: Don'ts and Dos

Draw your own warning sign, hold it up, and see if the class can guess what it is!

Example:

A: *What does this sign mean?*
B: *If you visit England, eat fish and chips!*
C: *No. If you visit England, practice English!*
A: *You got it.*

Segue

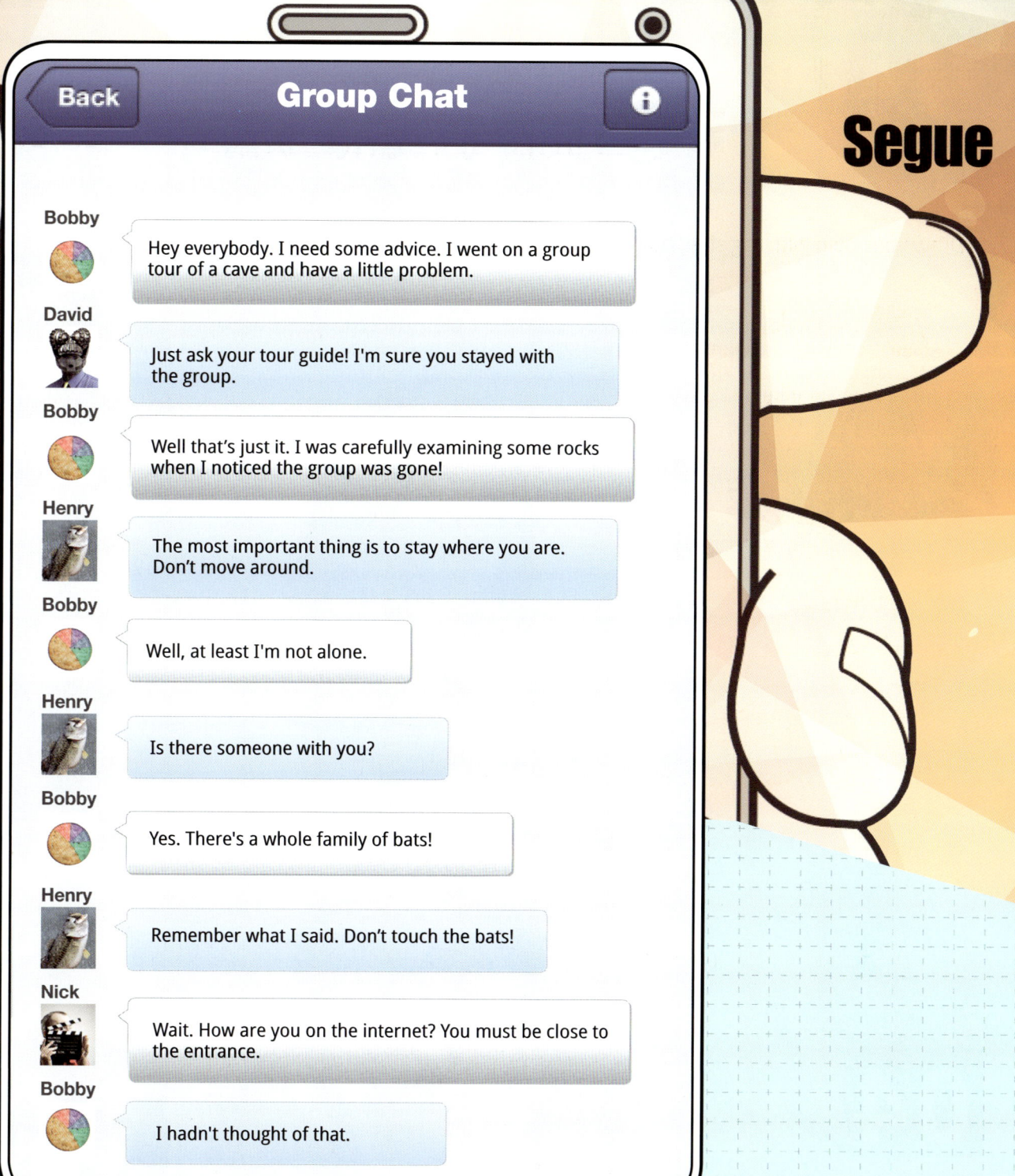

Group Chat

Bobby: Hey everybody. I need some advice. I went on a group tour of a cave and have a little problem.

David: Just ask your tour guide! I'm sure you stayed with the group.

Bobby: Well that's just it. I was carefully examining some rocks when I noticed the group was gone!

Henry: The most important thing is to stay where you are. Don't move around.

Bobby: Well, at least I'm not alone.

Henry: Is there someone with you?

Bobby: Yes. There's a whole family of bats!

Henry: Remember what I said. Don't touch the bats!

Nick: Wait. How are you on the internet? You must be close to the entrance.

Bobby: I hadn't thought of that.

A. Discussion
1. Have you ever been lost in a new place?
   - Did you ask someone for help or try to solve the problem yourself?
   - How long were you lost?
2. What are some things you would tell people to do or not do when visiting your country, city, or area?

B. Writing
Imagine someone is going to be taking care of your house for a week or taking over for you at your job while you are on vacation. Write a brief paragraph telling the person what to do.

Unit 3 Look Before You Leap | 67

04
It Takes All Kinds!
Impressions & Connections

Objectives:
/ Talk about your preferences in others
/ Listen to a dialogue about how someone seems

WARM UP

How would you describe...
- your best friend?
- your brother/sister?
- your pet?
- a co-worker you don't like?
- your teacher?

TONGUE TWISTERS

- I wish I were what I was when I wished I were what I am.

LESSON 1

A. Companion Type Quiz

• Asking about preference

Take this quiz to find out what kind of person is most compatible with you. This could be just a friend or perhaps a romantic interest!
> Ask a partner the following questions.
> Circle the answer that best connects to what you like in a companion.
> Give reasons why you would choose that kind of person.

Example:

A: *Do you prefer someone who is serious and thoughtful, sensitive and compassionate, or funny and outgoing?*

B: *I like someone who is sensitive and compassionate because I like to share my feelings.*

1
A. serious and thoughtful?
B. sensitive and **compassionate**?
C. funny and **outgoing**?

Do you prefer someone who is...

2
A. intelligent?
B. creative?
C. athletic?

Do you like someone who is...

3
A. cautious?
B. generous?
C. carefree?

Do you prefer people who are...

Compassionate (*adj.*): caring and kind
Outgoing (*adj.*): friendly; not shy

70 | SLE Generations 1C

4 Would you like him/her to look...

A. elegant and stylish?
B. **unique** and funky?
C. casual and **outdoorsy**?

5 When going on a trip, should he/she be...

A. organized and **punctual**?
B. curious and **flexible**?
C. extreme and daring?

6 When going out to eat, should he/she be...

A. healthy?
B. interesting?
C. adventurous?

7 Should he/she be...

A. quiet and **reserved**?
B. friendly and talkative?
C. loud and funny?

Score: A _____
Score: B _____
Score: C _____

Mostly A's	A's and B's	Mostly B's	B's and C's	Mostly C's
Type: The Provider	**Type:** The Professor	**Type:** The Artist	**Type:** The Romantic	**Type:** The Entertainer
Who is he/she? This companion likes to make a plan and would never break the speed limit.	**Who is he/she?** This person is intelligent. Likes to find out the answers to life's questions.	**Who is he/she?** This companion is creative. Loves to make things and go to new places.	**Who is he/she?** This person is charming. Enjoys communicating and sharing.	**Who is he/she?** This companion is playful. Wants nothing more than to have a good time.

> Does the person you chose from above sound like anyone you know?
> How are you similar to the person in the description? How are you different?

Unique (*adj.*): special; not ordinary
Outdoorsy (*adj.*): having a style matching outdoor activities
Punctual (*adj.*): on time, not late
Flexible (*adj.*): able to handle change comfortably
Reserved (*adj.*): Polite, not aggressive

B. Not Everything Is As It Seems

Language Point : Stating Impressions

Seem + adjective suggests that something is true, but you cannot be certain.
▶ *He seems very tall. In this picture he is taller than everyone else.*

◇Note: The verb *seem* makes an opinion sound less forceful and more polite.
You seem tired.

Pre-listening

Look at the pictures of Jack. Discuss with a partner which adjective goes best with the pictures of Jack.

Example:
A: *Jack seems hard-working.*
B: *Why do you think so?*
A: *Because he often studies late and falls asleep.*

- Adventurous
- Weird
- **Cautious**
- Lazy
- Sensitive
- Stressed
- Unique
- Outgoing
- Confident
- Hard-working

Listening TRACK 8-9

Ella went out on a date with Jack. She is telling her brother Nick about the date.
While listening, put an O next to the picture if your guess was correct. Put an X next to the picture if it was different.

Cautious (*adj.*): careful

Post-listening

With a partner, match the adjectives in the large circle to the people in the pictures. Then, find the opposite adjective in the small circle to the right of the pictures.

Example: Hard-working

A: *He seems hard-working. He's doing many things at the same time.*
B: *I agree. He's definitely not lazy.*

Self-centered (*adj.*): not caring about other people
Stingy (*adj.*): not liking to spend money
Pessimistic (*adj.*): having negative ideas
Introverted (*adj.*): shy; keeping thoughts and feelings inside

Unit 4 It Takes All Kinds! | 73

C. Too Cool for School

Discuss how different types of people would handle these situations. Ask your partner why he/she would do the things he/she says.

Hot-tempered / Even-tempered
a hot-tempered person do?
an even-tempered person do?
<u>you</u> do?

Adventurous / Cautious
an adventurous person do?
a cautious person do?
<u>you</u> do?

1. A taxi drives in front of your car. You have to brake hard not to hit it.
What would…

2. You can choose a week of ice climbing or a relaxing spa package for your next vacation.
What would…

Mellow / Energetic
an energetic person do?
a mellow person do?
<u>you</u> do?

Uptight / Relaxed
an uptight person do?
a relaxed person do?
<u>you</u> do?

Thrifty / Free-spending
a thrifty person do?
a free-spending person do?
<u>you</u> do?

3. You have the day off.
What would…

4. You have an appointment to meet a friend, but he is going to be thirty minutes late.
What would…

5. You win $1,000,000.
What would…

Conservative / Liberal
a conservative person do?
a liberal person do?
<u>you</u> do?

Optimistic / Pessimistic
an optimistic person think?
a pessimistic person think?
<u>you</u> think?

Loud / Soft-spoken
a loud person do?
a soft-spoken person do?
<u>you</u> do?

6. Somebody asks you on a date.
What would…

7. You receive a package. The note on the package says, "Open this. You deserve it!"
What would…

8. You get the best news of your life.
What would…

Adventurous (*adj.*): enjoying new, difficult, and/or dangerous things
Mellow (*adj.*): very calm
Uptight (*adj.*): nervous and sensitive
Thrifty (*adj.*): tight with money

Discussion Questions

1 What three adjectives would you use to describe your best friend?

   ▶ What three adjectives would your best friend use to describe you?

2 Do you think opposites attract? Why or why not?

3 What type of person makes a good husband or wife?

   ▶ What is terrible behavior for a husband or wife?

4 Which is more important to you, physical appearance or personality?

5 What are the most important qualities in a good co-worker?

   ▶ How about a good boss?

   ▶ How about a good employee?

6 Do people's personalities change as they get older?

   ▶ How have you changed?

7 What types of people do you try to avoid?

   ▶ What is one type of behavior you cannot stand?

8 What would you like to change about your own personality? Why?

LESSON 2

>> WARM UP

Objectives:
/ Expressing opinions of people and situations

How would you describe:
- something you bought recently?
- your last birthday?
- your mom's cooking?
- the last time you went out to eat?
- the best wedding you have been to?
- a great trip you took?

A. You're Not Boring

• True Conditions

Language Point: Verbs Used as Adjectives

Adding –ing to some verbs expresses opinions of situations and things. -ing adjectives have active meanings.
▸ *Today was an amazing day.* (The noun *day* is doing something)

Positive: Thrilling / Interesting / Exciting / **Amusing** / Surprising
Negative: Boring / Tiring / Embarrassing / Annoying / Depressing

Do You Remember?

- When we change a verb into an adjective using *–ed*, we use the adjective to talk about our feeling.

I feel bored today.
(bored is my feeling.)

PART 1 • Use the example sentences as a guide to create questions using the noun and verb that are given.

Example: Book / Confuse
A: *If a book confuses you, how do you describe the book?*
B: *It's a confusing book.*
A: *How do you feel?*
B: *I'm confused.*

1. Waterfall / Amaze

2. Event / Depress

3. Job / Tire

4. Movie / Bore

5. Painting / Interest

6. Situation / Embarrass

7. Person / Annoy

8. Episode / Surprise

9. Joke / Amuse

Amusing (*adj.*): humorous or entertaining

Unit 4 It Takes All Kinds!

PART 2 • How was it?
Based on the picture what do you think the event was like?

Tip: Be careful not to confuse verbs used as adjectives.
-ing describes an effect.
This test is terrifying. (scary)
-ed describes your feeling.
I am terrified.

1. Bungee jump
A: *How was the bungee jump?*
B: *It was so…*
A: *Why was the bungee jump _____?*

2. Final exam
A: *How was the big test?*
B: *It was really…*
A: *Why was the test _____?*

3. Fall trek
A: *How was the hike?*
B: *It was really…*
A: *What was so _____ about the hike?*

Possible Verbs

Freeze
Bore
Amaze
Exhaust
Worry
Terrify
Frustrate
Thrill
Excite
Depress
Interest
(Other)

4. Afternoon date
A: *How did your date go?*
B: *It was…*
A: *Why was it _____?*

5. Summer car race
A: *How was the race?*
B: *It was…*
A: *What made the race _____?*

6. Lantern festival
A: *How was the festival?*
B: *It was so…*
A: *What was _____ about it?*

Frustrate (v.): to cause someone stress due to difficulty or hardship

B. What Are You Made Of?

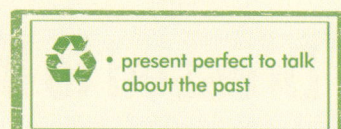
- present perfect to talk about the past

PART 1 • Have you ever...

> **Example:** had an embarrassing experience with a parent?
> **A:** *Yes, my mom always embarrassed me. She always sang pop songs in front of my friends.*
> **B:** *I think the most embarrassing thing a parent can do is...*

1 ...had an embarrassing experience with a parent?
- [ ] Yes? Why was it embarrassing?
- [ ] No? What is the most embarrassing thing a parent can do?

2 ...received really surprising news?
- [ ] Yes? Why was it so surprising?
- [ ] No? What is the most surprising news someone could tell you?

3 ...been to a really exciting event?
- [ ] Yes? What made it so exciting?
- [ ] No? What is the most exciting event you would like to see?

4 ...gone on a boring trip?
- [ ] Yes? Why was it so boring?
- [ ] No? What places would be too boring to visit?

5 ...taken an interesting class?
- [ ] Yes? What made the class so interesting?
- [ ] No? What is something interesting you would like to study?

6 ...done something extremely exhausting?
- [ ] Yes? Why was the work so exhausting?
- [ ] No? What is the most exhausting work you can imagine?

7 ...learned a very frustrating subject?
- [ ] Yes? What made it so frustrating to learn?
- [ ] No? What do you think would be a frustrating subject to learn?

8 ...been in a frightening situation?
- [ ] Yes? Why was it so frightening?
- [ ] No? What is the most frightening situation you can imagine?

PART 2 • Tell me a fascinating story about...

- a trip
- a night out with friends
- a time in school
- a date you went on
- something you heard in the news

C. Dressed to Impress

PART 1 ● **Choose your companion**

Choose one of the following people to hang out with for one day. Give reasons why you would spend time with him/her.

> **Example:**
> **A:** *Who would you like to hang out with?*
> **B:** *I'm going to hang out with Nancy. She seems cool, and I'm not uptight. I think we could get along well.*

Nancy

Good points:
adventurous, open-minded

Bad points:
pessimistic, **grouchy**

Likes people who are:
forgiving

Hates it when people are: uptight

Motto:
"Rock on!"

Chanthavong "Chan"

Good Points:
cheerful, optimistic

Bad Points:
hot-tempered,
too **sentimental**

Likes people who are:
generous

Hates it when people are: cold-hearted

Motto:
"Love conquers all!"

PART 2 ● **Plan your day**

> Take the person you chose out for a day.
> Think about him/her when you make your choices. Discuss why you choose what you do.
> You will be scored on your choice.

Choose one option for each time of day:

> **Example: Breakfast**
> **A:** *Where are you taking Nancy for breakfast?*
> **B:** *I want to eat donuts, but I don't think it will be adventurous enough for her.*
> *I'm going to choose the porridge. I think she'll be excited to try it.*

Bacon and eggs

Porridge and thousand-year-old egg

1 Where are you taking him/her for breakfast?

Donuts and coffee

Grouchy (*adj.*): bad tempered, in a mood to complain
Sentimental (*adj.*): affected by emotion easily

Jogging in the park

Sunbathing at the beach

Sushi bar

Indian curry buffet

2
Where are you taking him/her in the morning?

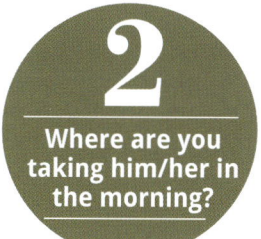
Horseback riding

3
Lunch

Barbecue cookout

Ice skating

Hang gliding

French restaurant with violin music

Japanese steakhouse with a chef at the table

4
Afternoon Activity

Chinese foot massage

5
Dinner

Sunset cruise

PART 3

Ask your partner how you did on your day out. Circle the number that corresponds to your score.

How did _____ like my choice for _____?

Name of Friend:			
Breakfast Score:	+1	0	-1
Morning Activity Score:	+1	0	-1
Lunch Score:	+1	0	-1
Afternoon Activity Score:	+1	0	-1
Dinner Score:	+1	0	-1
Evening Activity Score:	+1	0	-1
Total:			

Rodeo

Opera

6
Evening Activity

Salsa Dancing

Tell your partner(s) their scores for each option based on the choices they made. Find the score that connects to their choice (+1=great; 0=fine, but just so-so; -1=bad choice). After they calculate their score, read the result at the bottom.

Breakfast	Nancy	Chanthavong
Bacon and eggs	Nancy loves bacon and eggs. (+1)	Chan doesn't mind bacon and eggs. (0)
Porridge and thousand-year-old egg	Nancy is terrified of thousand-year-old eggs. (-1)	Chan is thrilled to eat thousand-year old eggs. (+1)
Donuts and coffee	Nancy is okay with coffee and donuts. (0)	Chan is tired of donuts and coffee. (-1)
Morning Activity	**Nancy**	**Chanthavong**
Jogging in the park	Nancy says jogging after a big breakfast is refreshing. (+1)	Chan jogs every day, but it's not the end of the world. (0)
Horseback riding	Nancy finds horses terrifying. (-1)	Chan is enchanted by horses. (+1)
Sunbathing at the beach	Nancy is not crazy about the beach, but it's fine. (0)	Chan had a bad experience at the beach. (-1)
Lunch	**Nancy**	**Chanthavong**
Indian curry buffet	Nancy loves spicy Indian food. (+1)	Chan thinks Thai curry is much better, but it's okay. (0)
Sushi bar	Nancy thinks sushi is **revolting**. (-1)	Chan thinks sushi is amazing. (+1)
Barbecue cookout	Nancy is okay with a cookout. (0)	Chan is scared of fire. (-1)
Afternoon Activity	**Nancy**	**Chanthavong**
Chinese foot massage	Nancy thinks a massage sounds fine. (0)	Chan is not thrilled with a massage, but it's okay. (0)
Ice skating	Nancy is embarrassed to go ice skating because she falls down too much. (-1)	Chan thinks ice skating is amazing. (+1)
Hang gliding	Nancy is thrilled to go hang gliding. It seems amazing! (+1)	Chan is terrified of hang gliding, it's how his grandfather died. (-1)
Dinner	**Nancy**	**Chanthavong**
Sunset cruise	Nancy loves the ocean. (+1)	Chan thinks a dinner cruise sounds a little boring, but if the food is good it's okay. (0)
Japanese steakhouse with a chef at the table	Nancy is terrified of knives. (-1)	Chan is always impressed by Japanese chefs. (+1)
French restaurant with violin music	Nancy has no problem with French food and violin music. (0)	Chan is broken-hearted because the love of his life moved to France. (-1)
Evening Activity	**Nancy**	**Chanthavong**
Rodeo	Nancy loves the rodeo. (+1)	Chan is not really interested in the rodeo, but he will go. (0)
Opera	Nancy is confused by the opera. (-1)	Chan always cries at the opera. It is so touching! (+1)
Salsa dancing	Nancy is into rock and roll, not Latin music, but she'll try it. (0)	Chan gets irritated and tries to kick other dancers. It's scary. (-1)

Score:

5 → 6	Gives you a copy of the keys to his/her house.
3 → 4	Wants to have a serious talk, and get to know you better!
1 → 2	Would like to hang out again some time.
0	Will be friends with you on MyFaceWorld.
-2 ← -1	Probably won't return your calls.
-4 ← -3	Tells you he/she will be out of town for a year.
-6 ← -5	Changes his/her phone number and moves to another town.

Revolting (*adj.*): creating feelings of disgust

Discussion Questions

1. When you are talking to a boring person, what do you do to make the conversation more interesting?

2. What types of people irritate you?
   - What **TV personality** annoys you?
   - Why is he/she so annoying?

3. What was the most confusing subject for you in school? Why was it so confusing?
   - Do you ever feel confused during English class? What confuses you?

4. In your opinion, what is the most entertaining program on television these days?
   - Why are you so entertained by this program?

5. What things are you most scared of?
   - Who is the scariest person you have ever met?
   - What is so scary about that person?

6. What would you do for a perfect day or night out?
   - Have you ever had a day like this? When?

7. Which things from activity C would you never try? Why?
   - Which activities would be too scary for you?
   - Which activities would be too boring for you?

UNIT 4 REVIEW

How well can you use…
- ☐ Ways to express impressions of others?
- ☐ Expressing your feelings about people and situations?

What do you need to study more?

TV personality *(n.)*: someone who appears regularly on TV

Activity: Extreme People

Time to invent a new person. He or she can be the **most interesting** person in the world, the **rudest** person in the world, or whatever you want.

I am going to create the _____ person in the world!

A. most interesting
B. most annoying
C. most humorous
D. rudest
E. smartest
F. most boring
G. most exciting
H. friendliest
I. (other)

- What will he/she <u>always</u> do?
- What things will he/she <u>never</u> do?
- What will his/her neighbors say about him/her?
- What will his/her former classmates say?
- What will his/her nickname be?

Example:

A: *Who is your person?*
B: *He is the most annoying person in the world.*
A: *What does he always do?*
B: *He <u>always</u> asks a lot of personal questions.*
A: *What does he never do?*
B: *He <u>never</u> stops talking on the phone.*

Last Ditch Dating.com

ONLINE DATING

Welcome to Last Ditch Dating.com

Register with us today

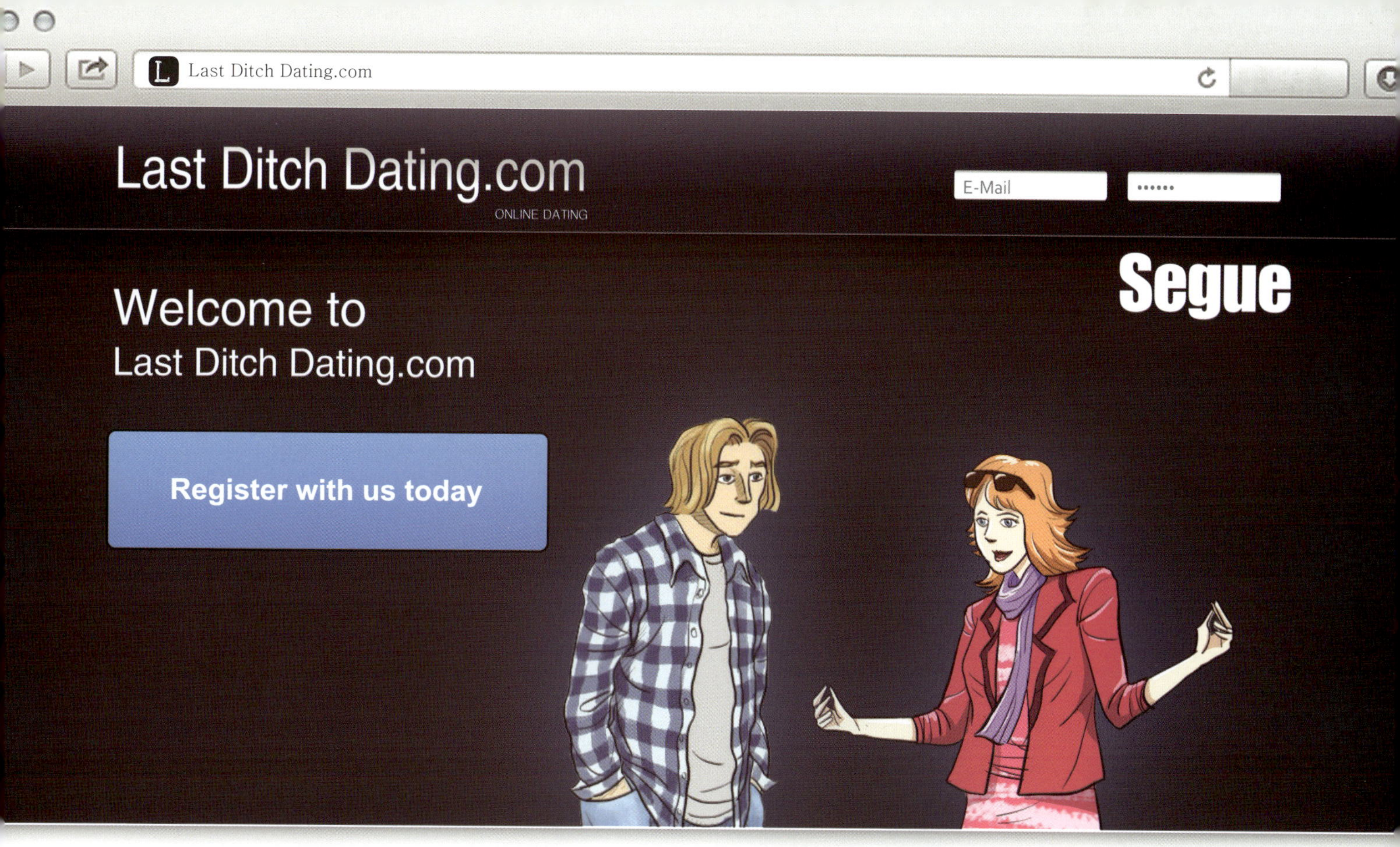

Profile
Name: Jack Thompson
Sex: Male
Age: 22
Blood Type: A
Job: Student. Senior at University of Learning

Personality:
Jack considers himself to be friendly and relaxed.
He's unique and adventurous.
He really likes working hard on his studies.
He isn't too proud, but he is self confident.
He doesn't think he's exceptionally attractive, but he doesn't think he's ugly either.

Profile
Name: Ella Jones
Sex: Female
Age: 21
Blood Type: AB
Job: Student. Senior at University of Education

Personality:
Ella considers herself to be very ambitious and wants to find a job soon after graduation.
She really likes adventure and hanging out with friends.
She is very friendly but can be a little too sensitive at times.
She feels confident that she is really attractive.

A. Discussion

1. Have you or anyone you know ever used an online dating website?
   ▶ What happened? Was the result good or bad?
2. Do you think people are truthful on online dating sites?
   ▶ What kinds of things might they lie about?

B. Writing

Write an online profile similar to the ones above for yourself or for someone you know. Be sure to highlight what you think the good things are about your/their personality.

Unit 4 It Takes All Kinds! | 85

05
X Marks The Spot
Location & Transportation

Objectives:
/ Practice describing locations
/ Listen to a dialogue about getting directions

WARM UP

1. Have you ever been asked to give directions? If yes, what happened?

2. Have you ever had to ask for directions? Where were you going?

3. What do you think the following signs mean?

LESSON 1

A. Street Scene

Language Point: Describing Outside Locations

On a street
▸ *My office is on Maple Street.*

Next to another location
▸ *It's next to Burger World.*

Between two locations
▸ *It's between Burger World and the hair salon.*

Across from–separated by a street
▸ *It's across from the park.*

Tip: We do not use "the" to describe our own home, work, or school.
Incorrect: *I'm at the home.*
Correct: *I'm at home.*

Language Point: Describing an Exact Location

At a specific location
▸ *It's at the corner of 3rd Avenue and Main.*
▸ *She's at the bank.*
▸ *We're at the bus stop.*

◇ Note: Use *the* before common nouns but not before proper nouns. *She's at Criswell Bank.*

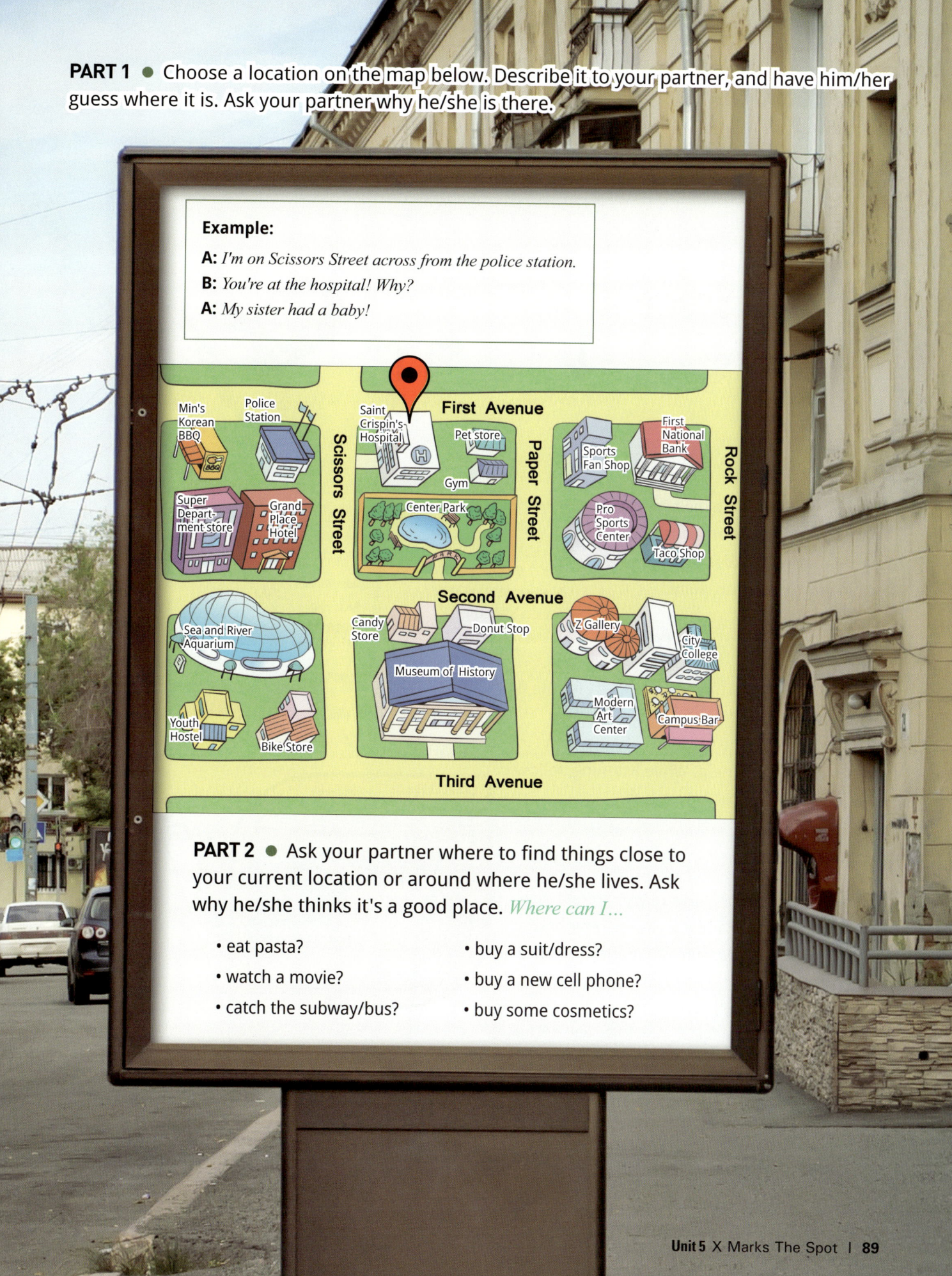

B. Get Lost

Language Point : Using Imperatives to Give Directions

Describing a direction:
go/head/walk:

west ←→ east
(back)   (straight)

up / north
↕
down / south

Changing directions:
turn / make a:

↰ ↱
left right

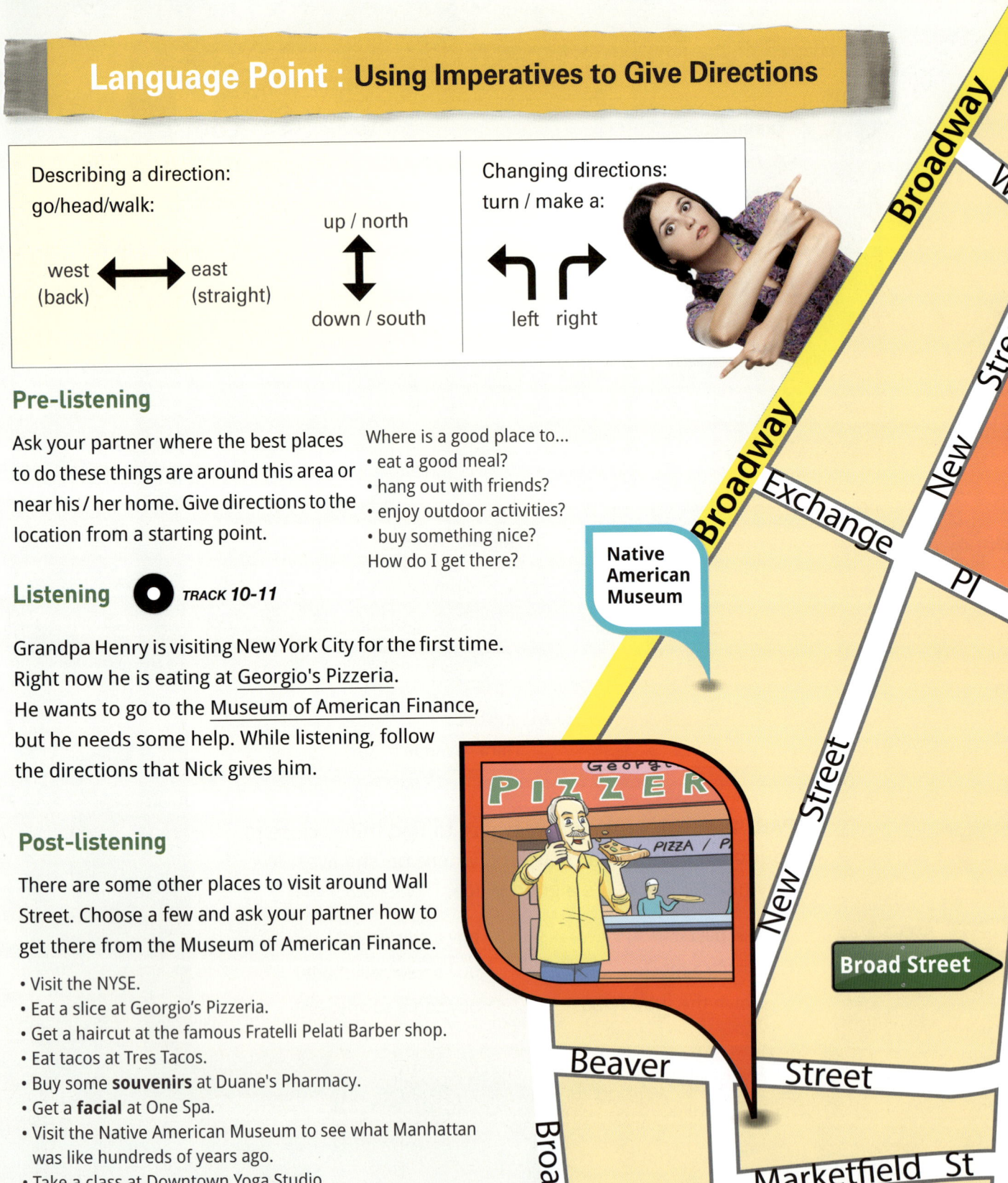

Pre-listening

Ask your partner where the best places to do these things are around this area or near his / her home. Give directions to the location from a starting point.

Where is a good place to...
• eat a good meal?
• hang out with friends?
• enjoy outdoor activities?
• buy something nice?
How do I get there?

Listening TRACK 10-11

Grandpa Henry is visiting New York City for the first time. Right now he is eating at Georgio's Pizzeria. He wants to go to the Museum of American Finance, but he needs some help. While listening, follow the directions that Nick gives him.

Post-listening

There are some other places to visit around Wall Street. Choose a few and ask your partner how to get there from the Museum of American Finance.

• Visit the NYSE.
• Eat a slice at Georgio's Pizzeria.
• Get a haircut at the famous Fratelli Pelati Barber shop.
• Eat tacos at Tres Tacos.
• Buy some **souvenirs** at Duane's Pharmacy.
• Get a **facial** at One Spa.
• Visit the Native American Museum to see what Manhattan was like hundreds of years ago.
• Take a class at Downtown Yoga Studio.
• Get a drink at Pearl Street Irish Pub.

Souvenir (n.): something bought to remind you of a place
Facial (n.): beauty treatment for the face

C. Poor Planning

PART 1 ● City Consultants have made plans for a new town called Cityville. Unfortunately, their ideas are terrible. With a partner or group, look at the following list of problems and discuss solutions.

Example: German, Swiss, and Austrian restaurants

A: Is it a bad idea to put these three restaurants next to each other?

B: They all make the same food. Let's move one across the river next to the hunting club.

1. Is it a bad idea to put a zoo across the river from the shooting range?
2. The rock concert hall is behind the retirement home. Is this the best place?
3. Is the sailing school in a good location?
4. Can you see any problems with the location of the children's playground?
5. Is this a good location for a fireworks store?
6. What's wrong with the high school's location?
7. What other problems can you see?

PART 2 ● With partners, make your own plans for a new town.

Where in the world would you like to locate this town?
_____

What kinds of factories and businesses would you like to build?
_____

What kinds of museums or tourist attractions would you open?
_____

What buildings do you need in the town for the local people?
_____

Discussion Questions

1. Do you have a good sense of direction or is it hard for you to find places?
   - Who do you know that has a really good **sense of direction**?

2. Is it easier to find places on foot or in a car? Why?
   - Is it easier to find a place using directions or reading a map?
   - Is it easier for you to use a GPS or a map?

3. What online services do you use for maps and directions?
   - When was the last time you got really lost? What happened?
   - Have you ever been abroad and couldn't access the internet for directions?

4. What are some major **landmarks** in your city? (famous buildings, towers, bridges)
   - What are some major landmarks in other cities you have visited?

5. Is it easy to get lost in your city? Why or why not?
   - Which neighborhoods in your city are most confusing?

6. Have you ever had anyone ask you for directions in English?
   - If yes, what happened?
   - If no, what would you do in this situation?

Vegetarian restaurant *(n.)*: a restaurant for people who do not eat meat
Retirement home *(n.)*: a place for elderly people who can no longer live alone
Garbage dump *(n.)*: a place that gathers large amounts of trash
Sense of direction *(col.)*: ability to know which way to go
Landmarks *(n.)*: famous places

LESSON 2

>> WARM UP

Objectives:
/ Talk about transportation
/ Give directions on transportation

1. How did you get to class today?
   > How far is it from your house to here?
2. After class, where are you planning to go?
   > How will you get there?
   > How far is it?
3. What's the best type of transportation for getting around your city?
   > What's the worst?

A. Trains, Planes, and Automobiles

PART 1 • Town and Country

Take turns asking the following questions. Be sure to ask follow-up questions.

1. Do you prefer the bus or the subway?
2. Do you think **fares** are expensive or cheap?
3. How often do you take taxis?
4. Where is the best place to take the train?
5. What things do you have to do on a bus or train? What can't you do?
6. What is the best way to see a new city?
7. What is the best thing about public transportation? What is the worst?
8. Have you ever been **cheated** by a taxi driver?
9. Have you ever been stuck on a bus or subway?
10. How would you change the transportation in your city?
11. Have you ever seen someone jump a **turnstile**?

Fare (*n.*): amount charged for a ride
Cheated (*adj.*): tricked by someone
turnstile (*n.*): entrance gate with metal bars that move in a circle

PART 2 ● Over the Sea

Take turns asking the following questions. Be sure to ask follow-up questions.

1 Do you like flying? Why or why not?
2 What things must you do before taking off in an airplane?
    • What things can't you do on an airplane?
3 Have you ever taken a cruise?
4 Have you ever used a car ferry?
5 What do you like about the airport?
    • What don't you like?
6 Do you get seasick?
    • What can a person do to avoid getting seasick?
7 Where would you like to fly?
8 What is more dangerous, a boat or a plane?
9 Do you like airplane food?
10 Have you ever traveled in first class?

B. Take the A Train

Language Point: Giving Directions on Public Transportation

Get on at / off at-
- *Get on the Orange Line at North Station.*
- *Get off at Central Station.*

Take (something) to-
- *Take the red line to Airport Station.*

Transfer to (something) / at (somewhere)-
- *Transfer to the shuttle at Airport Station.*

Tip: When giving directions, it's good to set a **boundary**:
If you _____ , you went too far.

Take the Blue Line to River Station.
If you pass Central Station, you went too far.

STUDENT A

You and your partner are at **Seaside** Station. You need to ask your partner how to get to the following places:

- Ferry Terminal
- Performance center
- Department Store
- Gallery Street
- Amusement Park
- Airport

Example: Airport

A: *Could you tell me how to get to the Airport?*
B: *Sure. Take the Blue Line one stop to Airport Station. Get off at Airport Station.*
A: *Thank you.*

You know the locations of these places:

1. Airport
2. Historic District
3.
4. Outdoor Market
5.
6. Zoo
7.
8. River Walk
9.
10. Palace Hotel
11.
12. City Tower

STUDENT B

You and your partner are at **Seaside** Station. You need to ask your partner how to get to the following places:

- Palace Hotel
- City Tower
- Zoo
- River Walk
- Historic District
- Outdoor Market

Example: Airport

A: *Could you tell me how to get to the Airport?*
B: *Sure. Take the Blue Line one stop to Airport Station. Get off at Airport Station.*
A: *Thank you.*

You know the locations of these places:

1. *Airport*
2.
3. Department Store
4.
5. Gallery Street
6.
7. Ferry Terminal
8.
9. Performance Center
10.
11. Amusement Park
12.

Boundary (*n.*): limit; line marking the end of something

C. The Great Escape

STUDENT A

PART 1 • You are the international jewel thief, Ruby Gone. You need to get back to your **hideout** in London, but you are being chased by Captain K.

• Choose one action in each step.

1 At Topkapi Palace in Istanbul,

A. go through the front gate.

B. go under the wall through a tunnel.

C. go over the wall.

2 Take _____ to Paris.

A. a plane

B. an overnight train

C. a river cruise

3 Take ...

A. a taxi to the Louvre Museum.

B. the subway to the Louvre Museum.

4 Inside the Louvre...

A. steal something from the Egyptian art exhibit.

B. steal from tourists in the lobby.

C. steal something in the French Painting Gallery.

Hideout (*n.*): a place where somebody is hiding

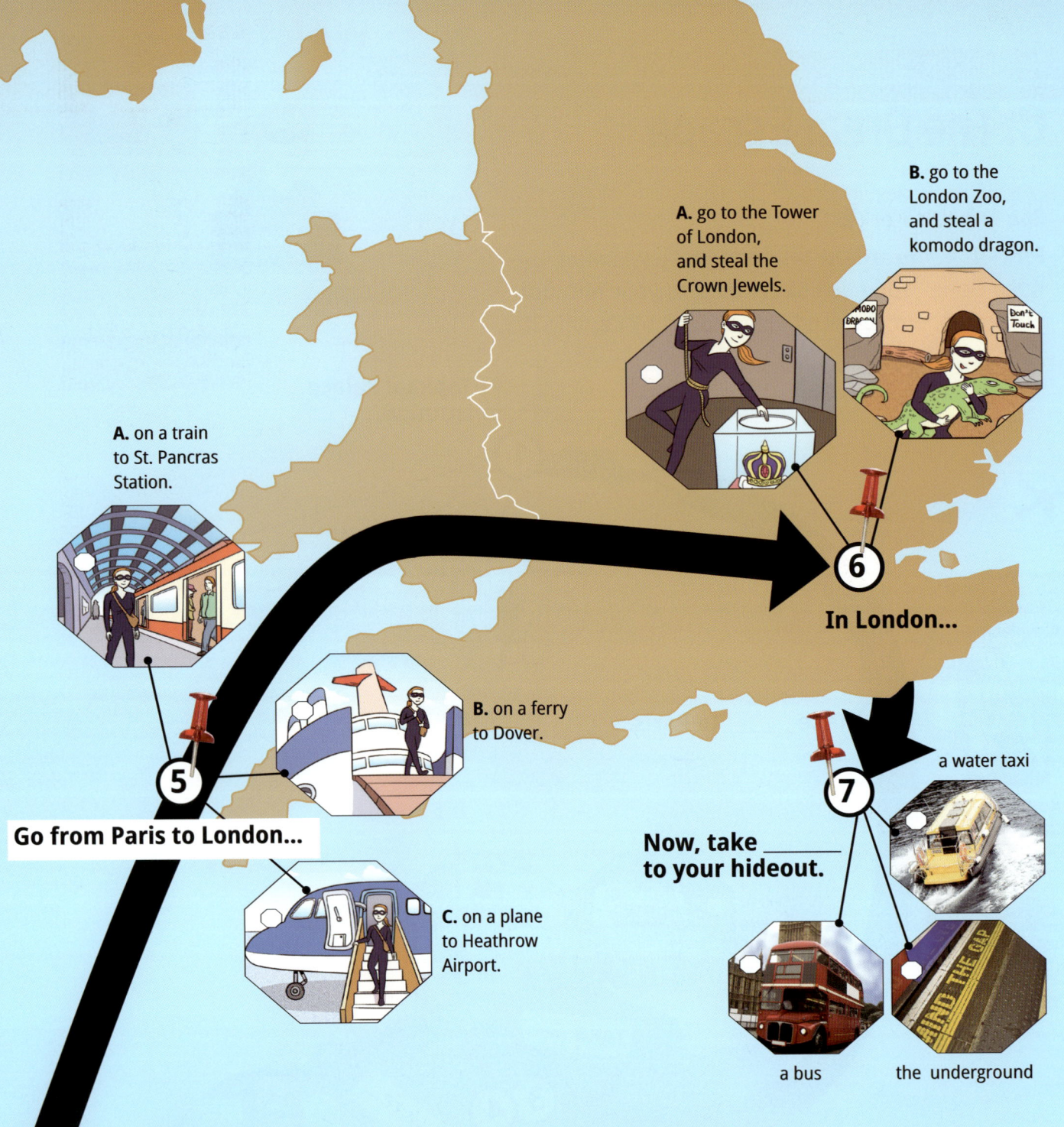

PART 2 • Answer Student B's questions about your location in each step.
If you and the detective are in the same place **4** times, he wins!
If the detective is in the same place as you less than **4** times, you win!

Example:

A: What did you do at the palace?
B: I went over the wall.
A: I waited next to the palace wall. I got you once! How did you get to Paris?
B: I took a...

WHEN YOU FINISH, SWITCH PLACES AND TRY AGAIN!

STUDENT B

PART 1

You are Atila Korkmaz of INTERPOL, but everybody calls you Captain K. You need to catch Ruby Gone, the international jewel thief, before she reaches her hideout.
• Choose one place to try and catch Ruby in each step.

At Topkapi Palace in Istanbul,
①

A. wait at the front gate.

B. wait in the tunnel under the walls.

C. wait next to the palace wall.

② **Take _____ to Paris.**

A. a plane

B. an overnight train

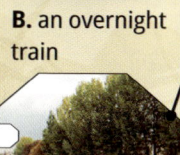
C. a river cruise

On the way to the Louvre,
③ ④

A. check all cars on the auto route.

B. check all passengers getting on the subway.

In the Louvre…

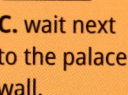
A. look in the Egyptian Art Gallery.

C. look in the French Painting Gallery.

B. look in the lobby.

Unit 5 X Marks The Spot | 101

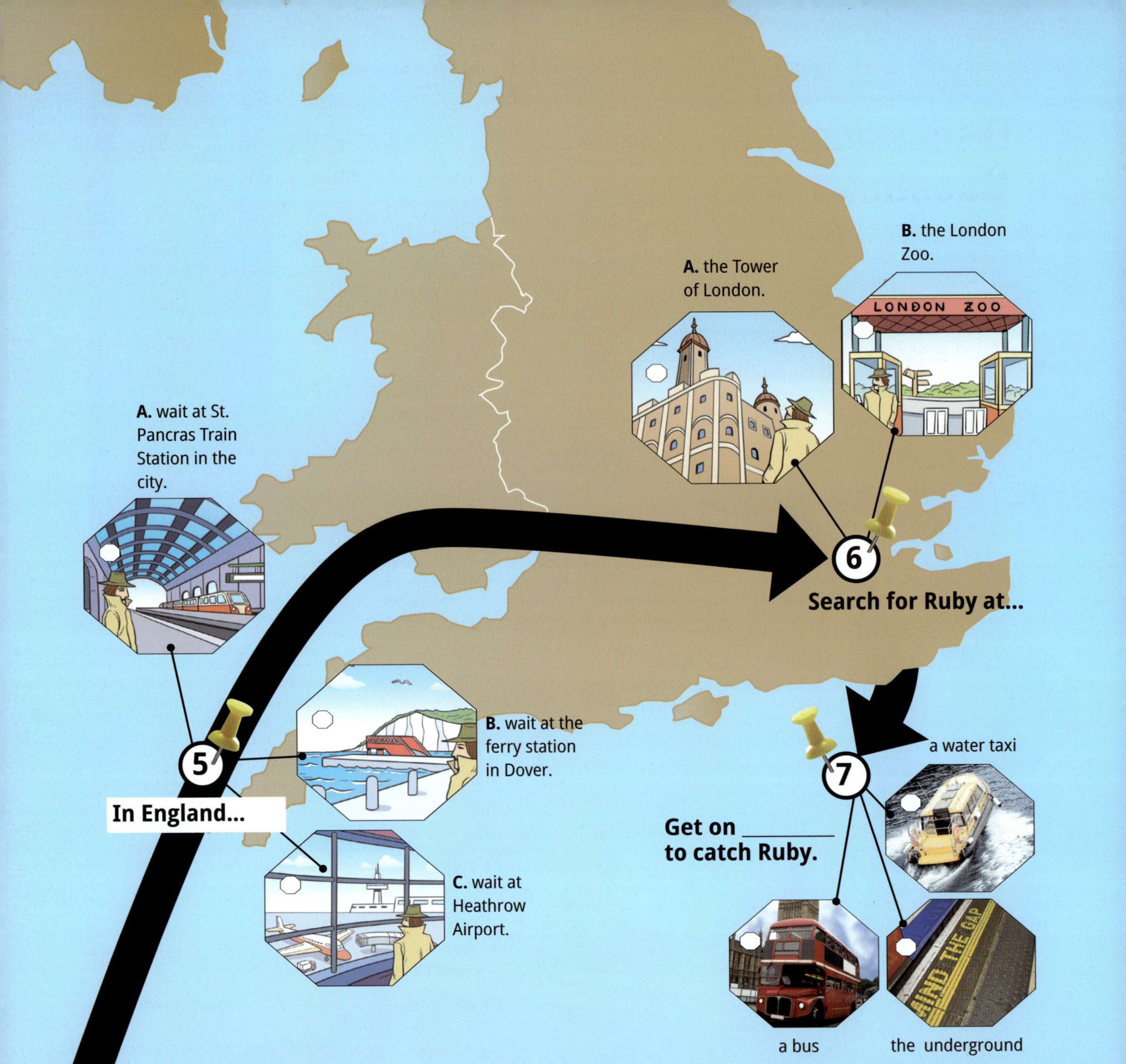

A. the Tower of London.

B. the London Zoo.

A. wait at St. Pancras Train Station in the city.

6
Search for Ruby at...

B. wait at the ferry station in Dover.

5
In England...

C. wait at Heathrow Airport.

7
Get on _____ to catch Ruby.

a water taxi

a bus   the underground

PART 2 ● Ask Student A what he/she did at each step.
- If you and Ruby are in the same place 4 times, you catch her!
- If you see Ruby less than 4 times, she escapes!

1. What did you do at the palace?
2. What did you take to Paris?
3. How did you get to the Louvre?
4. What did you steal?
5. How did you get to London?
6. Where did you go in London?
7. What did you take to your hideout?

Now, switch and try again!

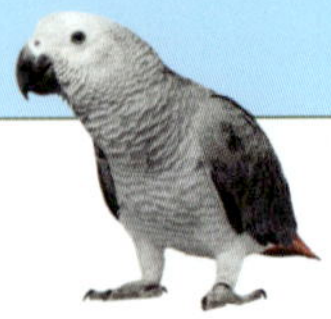

Example:

A: *What did you do at the palace?*
B: *I went over the wall.*
A: *I waited next to the palace wall. I got you once! How did you get to Paris?*

Discussion Questions

1 What is your **impression** of the following jobs?
   - Pilot
   - Bus driver
   - Taxi driver
   - Boat captain

2 Do you ever talk to people you don't know on public transportation? Why or why not?

3 Should people be allowed to sell things on public transportation? Why or why not?

4 What is your favorite area of your country to visit?
   - What is the best way to get there?

5 How has public transportation changed in your country in the last twenty years?
   - How would your city be different without public transportation?

6 How will public transportation change in the future?
   - Do you think space travel will ever be possible by public transportation?
   - Will we ever have self-driving cars?

7 Have you ever ridden a horse (or some other animal) for transportation?
   - If yes, what was it? Where were you?
   - If no, would you like to ride an animal? Which animal?

UNIT 5 REVIEW

How well can you use…
- ☐ Prepositions for describing location?
- ☐ Giving directions with imperatives?

What do you need to study more?

Impression *(n.)*: an opinion or feeling

Unit 5 X Marks The Spot | 103

Activity: Phrasal Movement

Match each picture to one sentence.

1. Ellie **went through** a hard time during high school.

2. Tony is going to **propose** to Grace. I hope she doesn't **turn him down**!

3. My son is a genius; he **came up with** several amazing inventions.

4. Lana says that she **came down with** the flu.

5. James got **kicked out** of the park because he didn't **go along** with the rules.

6. It's fine to make a **fashion statement**, but that couple **goes too far**.

Discuss the the following questions with a partner.

- The government wants everybody to stop using air conditioning during the summer. Would you go along with it? Why or why not?
- What is a fashion style that goes too far?
- What is the best idea a technology company has come up with in the past year?
- What should you do if you come down with a cold?
- What is a difficult experience you have gone through?
- Have you ever turned someone down when they asked for your phone number?

Propose (*v.*): ask to marry
Kick out (*phrasal v.*): to send somebody away
Fashion statement (*idiom*): an item of clothing that expresses a lifestyle

Henry'sTravels.blogopotamus

Segue

Hot Time, Summer in the City.

I'm finally in New York. It's my third day, and it's amazing!

I spent the first day in the Financial District. I saw the New York Stock Exchange, ate my first real New York pizza, and had a nice time at the Museum of American Finance.

Yesterday, I walked up Broadway to Worth Street, took a right, and spent the morning exploring Chinatown. I had lunch at a restaurant called Famous Sichuan. It was so spicy it almost made me cry, but it was delicious! After lunch, I got some ice cream. I then headed over to Columbus Park on Mulberry Street. Some locals taught me how to play a game called Mah-jong. I can't wait to teach the folks back home!

This morning, I wanted more exercise, but I was tired of walking. I took a taxi to the Downtown Boathouse, near Central Park. There, they have free kayak rentals! It was great. I went kayaking along the Hudson River.

A. Discussion

1. What are some unique neighborhoods like Chinatown in your city?
   ▶ What things are there to see or do there?
2. What traditional games do people in your country play?
   ▶ Do you think that people from other countries would enjoy learning to play them? Why or why not?

B. Writing

Write a simple travel blog entry like the one above about a place you have visited.
   ▶ What did you see there?
   ▶ What did you eat?
   ▶ Where did you stay?
   ▶ How did you get around?

06
I'm Glad You Asked
Reporting & Connecting

Objectives:
/ Reporting closed and information questions
/ Listen to a dialogue about being interviewed

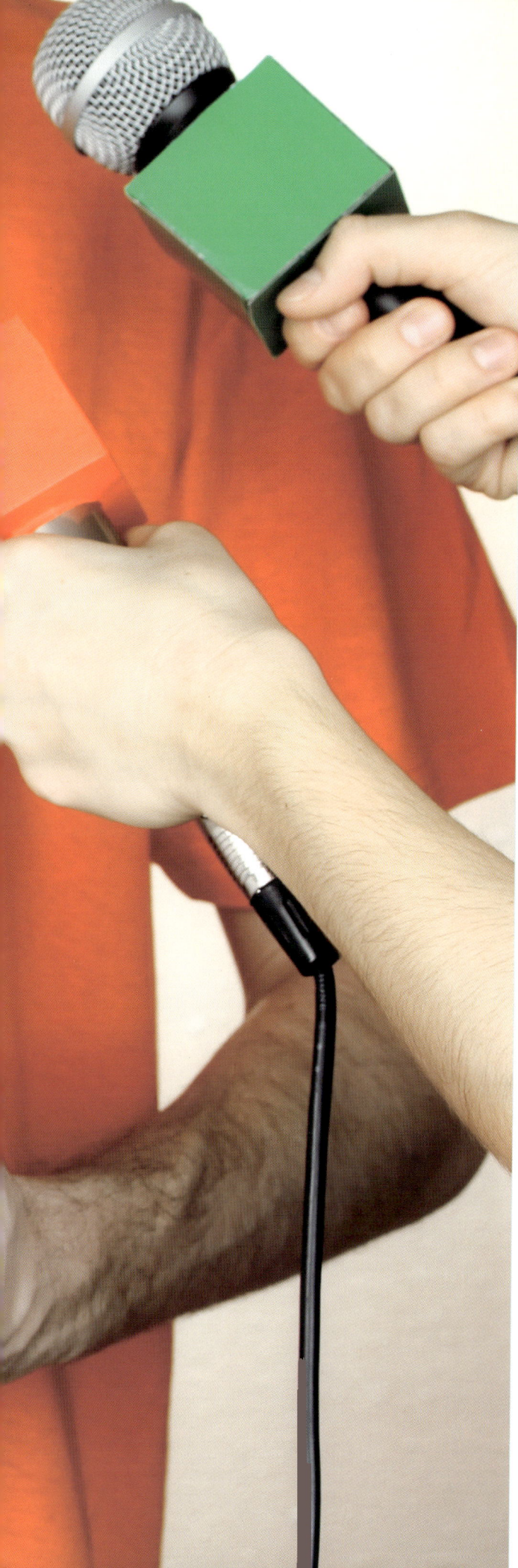

WARM UP

PART 1
What questions do you ask…
- someone you just met?
- someone you haven't seen in a long time?
- your parents?

PART 2
What questions do…
- your parents ask you?
- you hate answering?
- you think are really rude?

TONGUE TWISTERS

- Will you, William? Will you, William? Will you, William?
- Can't you, don't you, won't you, William?

LESSON 1

A. Yin / Yang

Are you a Type A or Type B personality?
Take the quiz to find out. Ask a partner the questions, and give reasons for your choices.
Circle the letter that is most like what you would do in each situation.

1 Your boss says you can't wear your suit on Casual Fridays. What do you do?

a. I ask my boss why she/he has a problem with my suit.
b. I say that I understand and that I'll wear something less fashionable next time.

2 A coworker asks you if he can look at your bag. What do you do?

a. I ask him why he doesn't have his own bag, and then I tell him to go away.
b. I say it's no problem, and I ask how his day is going.

3 A woman asks you if she can go to the front of the line at the bank. What do you say?

a. I ask her if she can go back and wait in line.
b. I say to go ahead and that it's no problem.

Neighbor (*n.*): person that lives next to you
Straightforward (*adj.*): very honest and clear
Passive (*adj.*): lacking positive action

❹ **A friend cooks dinner for you and it is terrible. What do you do?**

a. I ask him if he really expects me to eat it.
b. I say that it's good. I don't want to hurt his feelings.

❺ **A friend is having a party, but you really want to stay home. What do you say?**

a. I want to stay home and wash my dog.
b. I'll bring something to eat.

❻ **Your friend just got a terrible haircut. What do you say to him?**

a. I ask him who cut his hair.
b. I say that he looks just fine. I don't want to hurt his feelings.

❼ **Your neighbor asks you to help paint her house. How do you respond?**

a. I ask her if she's crazy.
b. I ask her what color she is painting the house.

❽ **Somebody calls you, and wants to ask some survey questions. What do you say?**

a. I say I don't have time and not to call back.
b. I ask her what kinds of questions they are.

❾ **Your neighbor asks you to turn down your music. How do you respond?**

a. I ask him why I have to turn it down.
b. I say I'm sorry and it won't happen again.

So, are you mostly A's or Mostly B's?

Type A
Assertive and **straightforward**, but sometimes a little too aggressive.

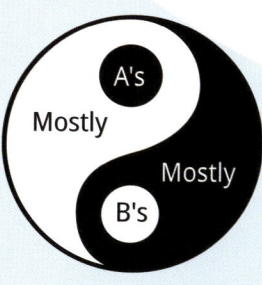

Type B
Laid back and cool, but sometimes a little too **passive**.

B. Ask Me If I Care

Language Point : Reporting Information Questions

When telling someone about a statement, use the verb *say*.
When telling someone about a question, use the verb *ask*.

A: *What did the teacher ask?*
B: *The teacher asked how my weekend was.*

◇ Note: When reporting, the verb in the question comes after the subject.
Subject: *my weekend*   Verb: *was*

Pre-listening

Think of an answer to three of the following questions:

1. Teacher: "Where do you live?"
2. Teacher: "When did you wake up?"
3. Teacher: "How did you get to class?"
4. Teacher: "What food do you hate?"
5. Teacher: "Who is your favorite singer?"
6. Teacher: "Why are you studying English?"

- Now ask a partner, "What did the teacher ask you?"
- First tell your partner one of the questions the teacher asked.
- Then, say how you answered.

Example:
A: *What did the teacher ask you?*
B: *She asked me where I lived. I said I lived in an apartment close to school.*

Listening TRACK 12-13

David was interviewed about an old student on the local news. He's telling Heather what happened.
Listen, and check the two things the interviewer asks David about.

☐ What is the student's name?
☐ Where does she live?
☐ How do you motivate your students?
☐ How often do you see her?
☐ Was she a really talented student?

Language Point: Reporting Yes / No Questions

When reporting Yes / No questions, add the word *if* before the question.

A: *What did she ask him?*
B: *She asked him if he was single.*

◇ Note: Just like with the verb *said*, the verb in the reported question is often in the past when reported later. Informally, you will also hear it in the present.
She asked if he's single.

Post-listening

Create two yes / no questions to ask a partner in each of the categories. Then, ask the questions to a partner.

Are you...?

1._____
2._____

Can you...?

1._____
2._____

Do you...?

1._____
2._____

Have you...?

1._____
2._____

Now, switch partners and tell your new partner what you were asked and how you responded.

Example: Are you having a good day?

A: *What did he ask you?*
B: *He asked if I was having a good day.*
A: *What did you say?*
B: *I said that I was having a good day.*

C. He Said / She Said

Arrange the pictures into one story. Explain the story using reported speech.

Example:
A: *What picture comes first?*
B: *I think the first picture is C. Patrick said that he loved Jamie very much. He asked if she would marry him.*

Discussion Questions

1. Have you ever told somebody that you liked their cooking when you didn't? Why?
   - ▶ Have you ever told somebody that they looked fine when they didn't look good? What happened?
   - ▶ Can you think of some other **white lies** similar to these? Explain.

2. What would you say to a stranger on the subway asking you for money?
   - ▶ Has this ever happened to you?

3. Have you ever asked somebody if they were married?
   - ▶ Have you ever asked somebody why they were not married?
   - ▶ Is this question polite, or is it too personal?

4. In your opinion, what is the most personal question someone can ask?
   - ▶ Do you know of any questions that are okay to ask in your culture but too personal in others?

5. How do you respond to telemarketing and phone surveys?
   - ▶ What do you say to the callers?
   - ▶ Have you ever responded positively to a telemarketing call?

6. In your opinion, is it alright to tell a person to be quiet?
   - ▶ What if the person is much older than you? Does it make a difference?

White lies *(idiom):* lies that are told to protect someone's feelings

LESSON 2

>> WARM UP

Objectives:
/ Talk about what was previously said
/ Make guesses about what others said

How important are the following problems for these couples?

A. Education
Howard has a university degree, but Kay doesn't. Is it okay?

B. Hobbies
Brooke can play video games really well, but Ahmed can't. He has no interest in games. Can they be a good couple?

C. Religion
Chris doesn't go to church, but Gina goes. Is that a problem?

D. Sense of humor
Mike is a joker, but Gemma isn't. She doesn't enjoy his humor. Is it okay?

E. Other
What other things are important for a couple to have in common?

A. Sew Dew Eye

Language Point : Similarities and Differences

Similarities-

+Positive statement	+Positive agreement
Pronoun + verb *I am hungry.*	**So + verb + pronoun** *So am I.*
-Negative statement	**-Negative agreement**
Pronoun + negative verb *I can't dance.*	**Neither + verb + pronoun** *Neither can I.*

◇ Note: Combine agreements using *and*.
I like cake, and so does she.

Differences-

+Positive statement	-Negative disagreement
I am hungry,	*but he isn't.*
-Negative statement	**+Positive disagreement**
I don't like strawberries,	*but he does.*

Enter the information in this simple Bio sheet. After you finish, compare what you wrote with your partner and talk about the similarities and the differences.

Example: Number of siblings

A: *How many siblings do you have?*
B: *I have two siblings, a brother and a sister.*
A: *So do I! But I have two sisters.*

Bio sheet

1. Sex: Male   Female
2. Number of siblings: _____
3. Favorite subject in school: _____
4. How did you come to class? (subway, bus, taxi)
5. What do you order at a café?
   ☐ (other)   ☐ americano
   ☐ cappuccino   ☐ latte
6. What kind of shoes are you wearing?
   ☐ dress shoes   ☐ sneakers   ☐ heels   ☐ sandals

Siblings (*n.*): brothers and sisters

B. Neither Snakes nor Ladders

> Get your partner's answer to the first question.
> Give your own answer to the same question.
> Make a correct similarity or difference statement, and move the right number of spaces.

A. Do you eat late at night?
B. Can you ice skate?
C. Are you **allergic** to anything?
D. Do you work out in a gym?
E. Can you **quack** like a duck?
F. Are you a good dancer?
G. Do you like horror movies?
H. Can you count to ten in French?
I. Are you afraid of spiders?
J. Do you wear contact lenses?
K. Can you stay awake for two days?
L. Are you interested in cartoons?
M. Do you watch baseball often?
N. Can you play the piano?
O. Are you from a small town?
P. Do you eat breakfast every day?
Q. Can you speak Chinese?
R. Are you a soccer fan?
S. Do you drink coffee?
T. Can you eat an entire large pizza?

Similarities	Move one space 1	Move two spaces 2	Move three spaces 3	Move four spaces 4	Move five spaces 5	Move six spaces 6
	So do I	Neither do I	So am I	Neither am I	So can I	Neither can I
Example Statement	You like pizza, and so do I.	You don't like Alfredo sauce, and neither do I.	You are afraid of spiders, and so am I.	You aren't interested in cartoons, and neither am I.	You can quack like a duck, and so can I.	You can't quack like a duck, and neither can I.

Differences	Move one space 1	Move two spaces 2	Move three spaces 3	Move four spaces 4	Move five spaces 5	Move six spaces 6
	But I can	But I can't	But I am	But I'm not	But I don't	But I do
Example Statement	You can't quack like a duck, but I can.	You can quack like a duck, but I can't.	You aren't interested in cartoons, but I am.	You are afraid of spiders, but I'm not.	You like pizza, but I don't.	You don't like Alfredo sauce, but I do.

Allergic (*adj.*): unable to eat, touch, or breathe something
Quack (*v.*): make a sound like a duck

Example: Do you eat late at night?

A: *Do you eat late at night?*
B: *No I don't. Do you?*
A: *Yes I do.*
B: *You eat late at night, but I don't.*
A: *Move five spaces.*
B: *Can you ice skate?*

If you land on the bottom of a ladder, go up to the top.

If you land on the head of a snake, go down to the bottom.

C. Don't I Know You?

Language Point: Confirming With Negative Questions

Negative questions are often used to check information.
- Don't you have school today?

(The speaker is asking: "You usually have school. Why are you not there?")

You can confirm the information.
- Yes, I do, but school was cancelled because of the snowstorm.

Or correct the information.
- Actually, it's winter vacation, so there is no school today.

Here are some incorrect statements. Discuss with your partner if you believe them or not, try to confirm the truth, and ask follow-up questions.

Example: Pizza is from Greenland.
A: *Pizza is from Greenland.*
B: *Isn't Pizza from Italy?*
A: *I think it is. Have you ever...*

1. Pizza is from Greenland. (is)
2. French fries are a healthy snack. (are)
3. Earth is the fourth planet from the sun. (is)
4. Watching television is good exercise. (is)
5. Ten plus ten equals 1010. (does)
6. The world is flat. (is)
7. Paper is from India. (is)
8. Coffee makes you sleepy. (does)
9. It is possible to lick your own elbow. (is)
10. February is winter in Australia. (is)
11. All snowflakes are the same. (are)
12. Santa wears a green suit. (does)
13. Thomas Edison invented the automobile. (did)
14. It is possible to fold a piece of paper in half more than seven times. (is)
15. People can only **hold their breath** for less than 15 seconds. (can)
16. The capital of _____ is _____. (is)

Hold your breath (*col*): wait and not breathe

Discussion Questions

1. What are three things you have in common with people in your family?
   (Example: My sister loves spicy food, and so do I.)
   - ▶ How about your friends?

2. What are three differences between you and your family?
   - ▶ How about your friends?

3. Do you go out in the sun often? How about your best friend?
   - ▶ Do you like cats? How about your best friend?
   - ▶ Are you an active person? How about your…?
   - ▶ Do you enjoy vegetables? How about your…?

4. Finish the following three sentences in your own way, and explain to your partner.
   - ▶ Nobody likes…, and neither do I.
   - ▶ Everybody is interested in…, and so am I.
   - ▶ Nobody can…, and neither can I.

5. Is a relationship bad if you always disagree with your **significant other**?
   - ▶ Is a relationship good if you agree about everything?

6. What are some things that all people have in common?

UNIT 6 REVIEW

How well can you use…
- ☐ Ways to report questions?
- ☐ Statements about similarities and differences?

What do you need to study more?

Significant other *(n.)*: husband, wife, or long term partner

Activity: Connection

One person should be the game host. The others can play on two teams. Make a true statement for each item on the chart using the following list:

Example:
A: *I'll take **"do"** for 100 points.*
B: *Cars use this, and so do motorcycles.*
A: *Uh, the road?*
B: *No! Guess again.*

CONNECTION!

	100	200	300
do	Cars use this, and so do motorcycles. √	Babies don't drink this, but adults do.	People don't have these, and neither do cats.
can	Birds can do this, and so can airplanes.	Humans can't eat this, but horses can.	Humans can't live there, and neither can whales.
be	Seoul is this, and so is London.	Taekwondo is this, but hotdog eating is not.	China is not this, and neither is India.

grass
beer
the Moon

gasoline √
horns
a capital city

an Olympic sport
fly
a South American country

Segue

Small Town Girl Solves Big Time Problem

By **Lawson D. Woods**, PNN

A local mathematician has solved the so-called "Happy Ending Problem". The problem was originally given its name because it led to the marriage of two prominent mathematicians.

Karen Smith, who went to Bridgemont high school, solved the famous theorem while studying at State University. Ms. Smith said she was first introduced to the problem by her math teacher, David Jones, in high school. "Mr. Jones showed us a list of unsolved equations when we were in his class. I really liked Geometry, and I often studied the problem on my own in my free time" she said.

When asked what he did to motivate his students, David Jones said, "I make math more interesting by showing students how it relates to their lives."

Ms. Smith tried to explain the theorem as easily

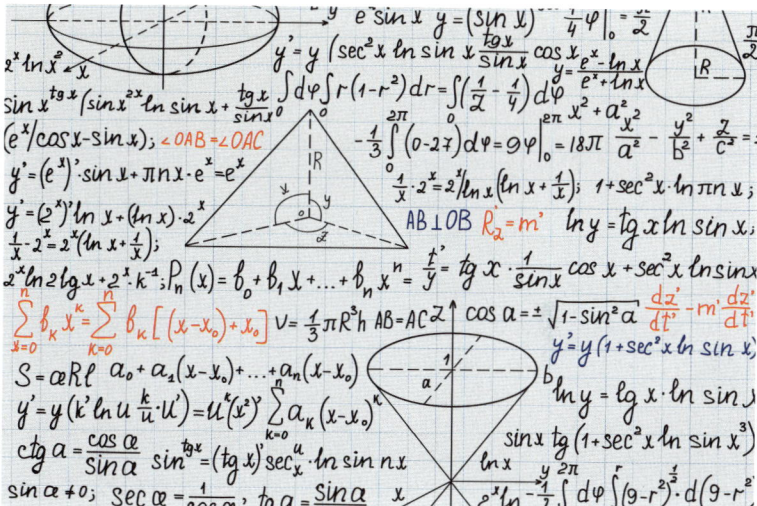

as she could, "The idea is that any set of five points has a subset of four points that form a quadrilateral." When asked how she solved it, she said, "The theorem can be proven by simple analysis, but I won't bore you with the details."

Mr. Jones said he was extremely proud and delighted that one of his former students had done so well. When asked if he remembered her, however, he said, "To tell you the honest truth, I can't put a face to the name!"

A. Discussion

1. Have you or anyone you know ever been interviewed by a newspaper or news reporter?
   ▶ If yes, what happened?
2. Would you consider it exciting or terrifying to be interviewed about a personal accomplishment?
   ▶ Would you like to be a news reporter? Why or why not?

B. Writing

Write a paragraph about a time you or someone you know was interviewed by the news.
▶ What happened?
▶ What did the news reporter ask?
▶ How did the person being interviewed respond?

07
The Real World
Existence & Speculation

Objectives:
/ Talk about existence
/ Listen to a dialogue about what a food consists of

WARM UP

PART 1

What is one thing you can only find...

- on this planet?
  (Example: You can only find humans on this planet.)
- on this continent?
  (Examples: a famous mountain; a country; a river)
- in this country?
  (Examples: a city; a company; a product)
- in this city?
- in this building?
- in this room?

PART 2

What do you think the proverb in the picture means?

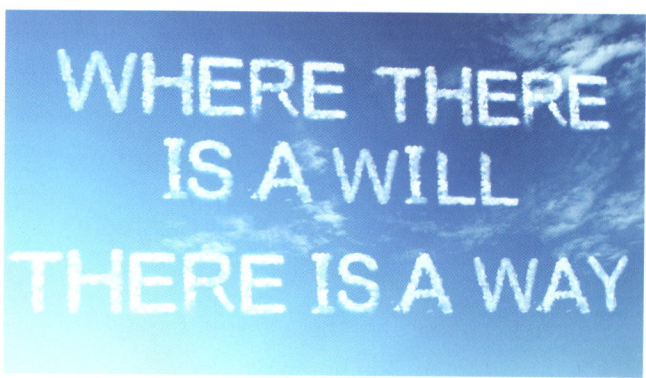

☐ "If you really want to do something, it is possible."

☐ "You will do something in the future at a specific place."

Unit 7 The Real World | 123

LESSON 1

A. There Is a Reason

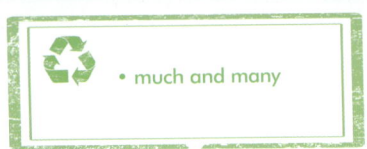
• much and many

Language Point : Talking About Existence

There + be is used to make questions and statements about existence and presence.

Are there + plural noun	Is there + singular or non count noun
Are there people outside?	Is there someone outside?
How many people are there outside?	Why is there someone outside?

◇Note: In statements, the main subject follows *there + be*.
There's something scary outside. (<u>something scary</u> is the subject)

PART 1 ● Answer the questions about presence with a partner.

1. How many people are there in this classroom?
   • *There are...*

2. How many people are there in your family?
   • Is there someone at home right now?
   (at your house/apartment)

3. Are there a lot of people outside on the street right now?
   • What are they doing?

4. What is your favorite area of the city?
   • What is there to do in that area?

5. What is the name of your favorite restaurant?
   • What is there on the menu?

6. Is there something you like to do to relax?

Soul mate (*n.*): another person that is the ideal match for a relationship

124 | SLE Generations 1C

PART 2 ● Ask your partner some questions about existence. Answer based on your opinion. Ask follow-up questions, and give reasons for your opinions.

Example: A soul mate
A: *Is there such a thing as a **soul mate**?*
B: *Yes, there is. I think some people match perfectly. What do you think?*
A: *Hmm. I'm not sure.*

Is there such a thing as...

1. a soul mate?
2. Santa?
3. easy money?
4. healthy fast food?
5. a perfect coffee?
6. bad weather?

Are there such things as...

1. best friends forever?
2. laptops that don't break?
3. aliens?
4. stress-free jobs?
5. ghosts?
6. honest politicians?

B. La-gag-me

Pre-listening

Discuss the ingredients in different kinds of prepared food. You can start the conversation with the following question:

Example: Kimchi

A: *How much garlic is there in kimchi?*
B: *There's a lot of garlic in kimchi.*
A: *Is there milk in it?*
B: *There's no milk in it.*
A: *How about sugar?*
B: *There is some sugar in it but not much.*

How much...(ingredient)...is there in...(prepared food)?

Ingredients
salt
pepper
milk
sugar
wheat
meat
(other)

Prepared Foods
kimchi
ice cream
spaghetti
cereal
sausage
ketchup
(other)

No salt	A bit of salt (a little salt)	Some salt	A lot of salt	Nothing but salt

Listening TRACK 14-15

Ella, Bobby, and Nick are enjoying Grandma's lasagna, but something seems different. Check off the ingredients they talk about. Then, choose the correct "secret ingredient."

Language Point : "On it" vs. "In it"

Use *on it* if the ingredient stays on a surface.
▸ *The pizza has cheese and spinach on it.*

Use *in it* if the ingredient goes into a mixture.
▸ *The pizza has tomato sauce in it.*

Post-listening

Discuss your food preferences using the dishes and ingredients below. Which do you like most? Which would you like to try?

Example:
A: *In France, people often eat pizza with eggs on it. Would you like that?*
B: *That sounds pretty good. How about pizza with honey on it?*
A: *That's too sweet for me. I like honey in tea, not on pizza!*

Ingredients:

Seafood

Broccoli

Cheese

Tomatoes

Mustard

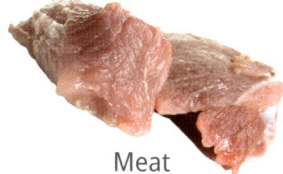
Meat

Eggs

Fruit

(other)

Onions

Dishes: Pizza
Pasta
Soup
Sandwiches
(other)

C. Rally to Table Mountain

On Table Mountain, there is a goat who knows winning lottery numbers. You and your partner have to get there before someone else does.

1. First, choose a car to get you there.

The blue car (can get one item delivered from the shop)

The yellow car (can skip one **obstacle**)

2. Before you go, choose 6 items to take with you:

A **A jackhammer**
to smash rocks

B **A crane with arms**
to pick up **logs**

C **Super bright lights**
to get through dark places

D **A lightning rod**
for **deflecting** lightning

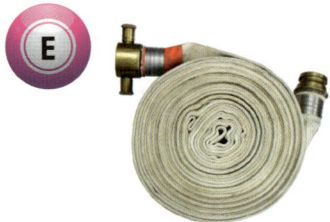

E **A fire hose**
for cooling down hot surfaces

F **A jet engine**
for jumping off ramps

G **Boards**
for making a temporary bridge

H **A flotation device**
for driving through deep water

I **A magnetic crane**
to move heavy metal objects

Enter the letters that you chose in the box on the map.

Obstacle (*n.*): a thing that makes it hard to move in one direction
Deflect (*v.*): make something change direction
Logs (*n.*): cut trees

One student keeps the previous page open, and the other student keeps this page open.

1. You can't go through the tunnel unless you have some bright lights. Are there super bright lights in your car?
   - Yes, there are. (Go to number 6.)
   - No, there aren't. (Go to number 2.)

2. There's an open manhole in the road. Is there a magnetic crane in your car to move the cover onto the hole?
   - Yes, there is. (Go to number 5.)
   - No, there isn't. (Go to number 3.)

3. There are rocks all over the road. Is there a jackhammer in your car?
   - Yes, there is. (Go to number 6.)
   - No, there isn't. (Go to number 4.)

4. There are logs all over the road. Is there a crane with arms in your car?
   - Yes, there is. (Go to number 6.)
   - No, there isn't. (Go to number 5.)

5. There's a ramp over the volcano. Is there a jet engine in your car?
   - Yes, there is. (Go to number 10.)
   - No, there isn't. (Go to number 4.)

6. There's a bad lightning storm ahead. Is there a lightning rod in your car?
   - Yes, there is. (Go to number 7.)
   - No, there isn't. (Go back through the tunnel to number 3.)

7. There's dangerous lava on the road. Is there a fire hose in your car?
   - Yes, there is. (Go to number 8.)
   - No, there isn't. (Go to number 5.)

8. There's a giant gap in the road at the snack shop. Are there boards in your car to get over it?
   - Yes, there are. (Go to number 9.)
   - No, there aren't. (Trade one item from your car with the snack shop, and go to 9.)

9. There's construction ahead. Is there a magnetic crane or a crane with arms in your car to help get the road cleared?
   - Yes, there is. (Go to number 10.)
   - No, there isn't. (Go back to the tool shop. Fail.)

10. There's a flood covering the road. Is there a flotation device in your car?
    - Yes, there is. (You are a big winner!)
    - No, there isn't. (Use your special ability if you have it. Otherwise, you sink.)

The winning numbers are:

Three, five, eiiiiiight....

Manhole (*n.*): a hole in the street used for underground work
Lava (*v.*): hot liquid from a volcano

Discussion Questions

1. How much money is there in your wallet at the moment?
   - How many pictures are there on the wall in your home?
   - What pictures are on the money in your country?

2. Is there such a thing as getting something for nothing?

3. Is there a way to…
   - change the color of your eyes?
   - make everybody like you?
   - look young forever?
   - make children want to study?

4. What interesting things are there to see and do in your city?
   - How about in other cities in your country?
   - How about in your favorite foreign country?

5. What ingredients are there in your favorite…
   - dish?
   - drink?
   - dessert?

6. How many people are there…
   - in your family?
   - in your group of friends?
   - in your school or at your job?

LESSON 2

>> WARM UP

Objectives:
- Talk about certainty
- Make guesses based on what you know

What percent possibility is there of the following things happening to you?

> Getting married
> Going on vacation soon
> Owning your own company
> Getting lost this week
> Seeing your best friend
> Eating something delicious
> Learning something new

A. Nothing's For Certain

Language Point : Degrees of Certainty

Where's Johnny?

50% sure or less — **95%** sure → **100%** sure

may / might + verb
He might be sick.

must + verb
*He must be sick.
He always comes.*

verb
He's sick. I talked to him earlier.

PART 1 • Take turns asking the questions with a partner. Use *must* in your answers. If you are 100% sure, use *be*.

1. A: *Why is Clare yawning?*
   B: *She must be...*
   A: *What is she doing?*
   B: *She must be...*
   A: *Why do you think so?*

2. *How do the fans feel? What team are they supporting?*

3. *How does Mike feel? Do the two girls know each other?*

4. *What is Jared doing? Where is he?*

PART 2 • Take turns asking questions with a partner. Use *may* or *might* in your answers.

1. What does your teacher like to do on weekends?
2. What do you think I have in my bag/pocket?
3. What brand of cell phone do most of our classmates have?
4. What is your favorite actor doing right now?
5. How often do you think I go to (part of the city)?

Example:

A: *Our teacher must study all weekend. He's so serious.*

B: *He might go to a café on weekends. He loves coffee.*

Language Point : Negative Degrees of Certainty

Is Danny hungry?

- **100% sure** — not + verb
  He isn't hungry.
  He said he was full.
- **99% sure** — can't / must not + verb
  He can't be hungry.
  I saw him eat a whole pizza.
- **50% sure or less** — may / might not + verb
  He might not be hungry.
  He usually eats before class.

PART 3 • Look at the pictures, and answer the questions based on what you can see.

1. Is Jenny in Bangkok?
She _____ in Bangkok because...

2. Is David lost?
He _____ lost because...

3. Is Timmy **drowning**?

4. Is Karen happy with her diet?

5. Is Spike hurting Socks?

6. Is Jenny buying that sweater?

7. Is Joel a good driver?

8. Is Gretchen okay?

9. Is Barney fully awake?

Drown (v.): to die under water

B. What-sa-ma-jig

> Give your partner hint A, and let him/her guess what it is.
> If he/she cannot guess what it is, give hint B.
> If he/she still cannot guess what it is, explain what the item is made of and used for.

♻ · made of and used for

Example: Television
A: *You might use this every night.*
B: *It might be a computer.*
A: *No, it's not that. It is made of plastic and glass. It is used for entertainment.*
B: *It must be a TV.*

STUDENT A

Give these hints to your partner:

A. You can't use this without putting something inside.
B. You might use this to connect two pieces of paper.

1. **Stapler**

A. You might get paper from this.
B. You might not have one unless you work in an office.

3. **Photocopier**

A. You might use this at school or work.
B. You may need to charge this frequently.

2. **Laptop**

A. There might be one of these above you.
B. You might not use this in the day time.

4. **Light Bulb**

A. You might need this to be comfortable.
B. You might not use this in October.

5. **Air Conditioner**

A. You keep something inside this.
B. You might pay a fee to use this.

6. **ATM**

A. You may have one in your kitchen.
B. You might never use it, but you need it.

7. **Fire Extinguisher**

A. You might need this in school.
B. You might not be allowed to use it during a test.

8. **Calculator**

You are getting clues about these items:

- Rice Cooker
- Fan
- Mechanical Pencil
- Washing Machine
- Microwave
- Vacuum
- Mouse
- Watch

Unit 7 The Real World | 135

> Give your partner hint A, and let him/her guess what it is.
> If he/she cannot guess what it is, give hint B.
> If he/she still cannot guess what it is, explain what the item is made of and used for.

Example: Television
A: *You might use this every night.*
B: *It might be a computer.*
A: *No, it's not that. It is made of plastic and glass. It is used for entertainment.*
B: *It must be a TV.*

STUDENT B

Give these hints to your partner:

1. A. You might fill it every day.
   B. You might burn yourself, if you're not careful.

   Rice Cooker

2. A. You may not have one at home.
   B. You might use this to do something quickly.

   Microwave

3. A. You might use this about once a week.
   B. You may need this after being in a smoky place.

   Washing Machine

4. A. You might use this to dry things.
   B. You may not use it in the winter.

   Fan

5. A. You might have one of these with you.
   B. You might need to fill it often.

   Mechanical Pencil

6. A. You might plug it in, but you might not.
   B. It might not work on glass.

   Mouse

7. A. You may wake up your neighbors using this late at night.
   B. You might use this after spilling something.

   Vacuum

8. A. You might use it to remind you of something.
   B. You might not like them.

   Watch

You are getting clues about these items:

- Laptop
- ATM
- Light Bulb
- Air Conditioner
- Fire Extinguisher
- Photocopier
- Stapler
- Calculator

C. Around the World In The Rest of Today

PART 1 ● You have won a trip to fly around the world! There are some rules however:
> You can only go to five cities from the map below.
> Choose your starting city.
> You must always fly <u>east</u>. You cannot fly <u>west</u>. (But you can fly across the Pacific.)
> You only have time to see the four places listed in each city.

Write your cities from west to east below (Don't show your partner(s)):

①   ②   ③   ④

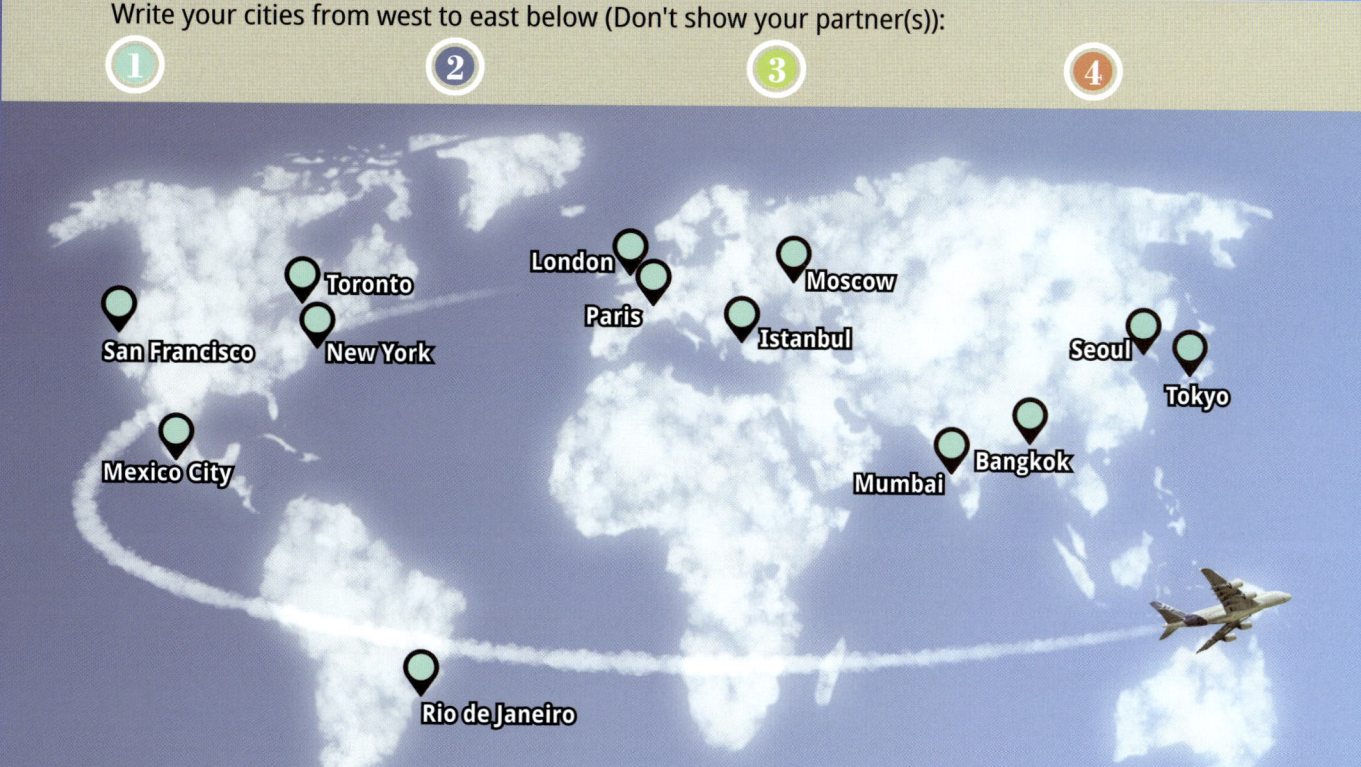

WEST   **EAST**

You can ask **three** questions to find out what city your partner is in. Use this conversation as a guide.

Example: San Francisco

A: *What is there in your first city?* (1st open question)

B: *There is a famous bridge.* (Only answer with one thing from the list.)

A: *What else is there?* (2nd open question)

B: *There is a large park.* (Only answer with one thing from the list.)

A: *Is there a Chinatown?* (3rd specific question)

B: *Yes, there is!*

A: *You must be in San Francisco.* (Make a guess)

B: *You got it!* (Move onto the next city)

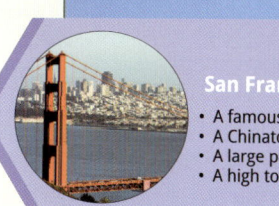

San Francisco
- A famous bridge
- A Chinatown
- A large park
- A high tower

Mexico City
- A large square
- An old cathedral
- Ancient pyramids
- Traditional markets

Toronto
- A high tower
- A Chinatown
- An arts district
- A famous shopping center

Unit 7 The Real World | 137

New York
- A famous statue
- Famous museums
- A large park
- A ChinaTown

Rio de Janeiro
- A famous statue
- An old cathedral
- A great beach
- A mountain overlook

London
- A famous bridge
- A big river
- A historic castle
- A palace

Paris
- A high tower
- An old cathedral
- A big river
- Famous museums

Istanbul
- A famous bridge
- An old mosque
- A palace
- Traditional markets

Moscow
- A large square
- A big river
- An opera house
- An old cathedral

Mumbai
- A great beach
- An old mosque
- An arts district
- Traditional markets

Bangkok
- A palace
- A big river
- A famous statue
- A ChinaTown

Seoul
- A high tower
- A palace
- A big river
- A famous statue

Tokyo
- A mountain overlook
- A high tower
- A palace
- Famous seafood

PART 2

1. Which of the cities from the activity have you been to?

2. Which of the cities haven't you been to?

Optional: Play again, but this time you can only ask **two** questions:

1. What is there in the city?
2. Is there a _____?

Discussion Questions

1. Some people say that the pyramids in Egypt might be the work of space aliens. What is your opinion?
   ▶ Are there any other mysterious places in the world that you know about?

2. What might you be doing at this time…
   ▶ next week?
   ▶ next year?
   ▶ ten years from now?

3. What is your _____ doing right now?
   ▶ dad   ▶ mom
   ▶ best friend   ▶ pet

4. Which team might win the next World Cup?
   ▶ Will your country's team do well in the next World Cup?

5. When was the last time you listened to a story and thought the person might be lying?
   ▶ What happened?

6. What is a job that might make a person very rich?
   ▶ What is a job that must be a lot of fun?
   ▶ What is one job that must be really hard?

UNIT 7 REVIEW

How well can you use…
☐ There + be to discuss existence?
☐ Ways to express certainty?
What do you need to study more?

Activity : Landmarked

With your partner, see how many of the landmarks you can place in the cities from Activity C.

- Golden Gate Bridge
- Notre Dame 
- Central Park 
- Red Square 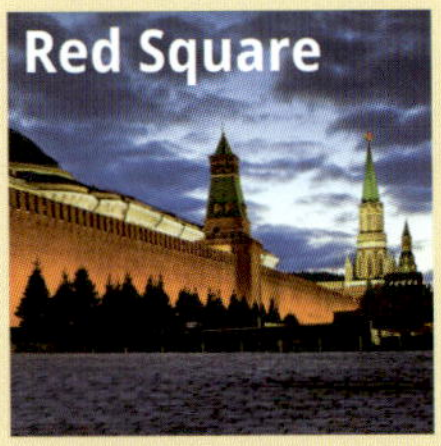
- Buckingham Palace 
- Copacabana Beach 
- Distillery Arts District 
- Reclining Buddha
- Pyramid of the Sun 
- Haji Ali Mosque  
- The Grand Bazaar
- Admiral Yi Sun-Shin
- Edo Castle 

Can you think of the name of another famous monument or area in one of the cities?

FusionRecipes.com

Fusion Recipes

Segue

| food | health & beauty | people features | reviews of my favorites | what's new | about | ▼more |

Ruth's Thai Chili Peanut Butter Lasagna

I combined one of my best dishes, lasagna, with some new ingredients I learned about in my Thai cooking class. I hope you enjoy it as much as my grandkids did!

Search Lasagna

Ingredients:

Meat:
500 grams of ground beef

Vegetables:
1 chopped carrot
1 piece of chopped celery
1/2 chopped onion
chopped parsley
chopped basil
5 Thai chili peppers
5 large tomatoes
4 cloves of garlic

Cheese:
250 grams ricotta cheese

Other:
1/2 tablespoon black pepper
Salt to taste
150 ml tomato paste
200 ml peanut butter
1 egg
1 tablespoon olive oil
8 large lasagna noodles

1. Mix the ricotta cheese and the egg.
2. Heat the olive oil in a frying pan, and cook the garlic for about 30 seconds.
3. Add the meat, and cook for about 2 minutes. Stir often.
4. Add the onions, carrots, and celery, and cook for 2 more minutes.
5. Add the remaining vegetables and other ingredients (including the peanut butter). Turn down the heat, cover the pan, and cook for 1 hour.
6. Boil lasagna noodles in a pot for about 10 minutes.
7. Put 1/3 of the meat sauce in the bottom of a baking pan. Put four lasagna noodles on top of the sauce, and put 1/3 of the cheese mixture on top of the noodles.
8. Put the remaining sauce and cheese on top.
9. Bake in the oven at 190 degrees for about 40 minutes.

A. Discussion

1. Do you think you would like this lasagna?
   ▶ What would you change about it?
2. What is the most surprising fusion dish you have tried?

B. Writing

Write a short recipe like the one above that combines two interesting or different foods.

WARM UP

A. With your classmates, brainstorm a list of jobs that you think are really important.

B. Which of the jobs you brainstormed…

- are high paying?
- are dangerous?
- need a lot of education?
- have long working hours?
- are usually done by men?
- are usually done by women?
- would you never do?

TONGUE TWISTERS

- How many cookies could a good cook cook if a good cook could cook cookies?
- A good cook could cook as many cookies as a good cook who could cook cookies.

LESSON 1

A. Who Are the People in Your Neighborhood?

Language Point : *Good at* to Describe Skills

good at + noun	▶ *He is good at chemistry.*
good at + gerund (verb + ing)	▶ *He is good at solving problems.*

With a partner, look at the occupations on the next page. For each occupation, discuss the following questions:

- What does a _____ do?
- Where does a _____ work?
- What is a _____ good at?

Example: Doctor

A: *What does a doctor do?*
B: *A doctor takes care of patients.*
A: *Where does a doctor work?*
B: *A doctor usually works at a hospital or clinic.*
A: *What is a doctor good at?*
B: *A doctor is good at communicating with patients.*

Workplaces: *A _____ works...*

At	In	On
at a hospital	in the city	on a farm
at a company	in the countryside	on a plane
at a school	in a classroom	on a construction site
at a bank	in the IT department	on the runway
at home	in the meat department	on a photo shoot
at a market	in a bar	

144 | SLE Generations 1C

Occupations:

Server, Construction Worker, Taxi Driver, Butcher, Teacher, Police Officer, Fashion Model, Florist, Custodian, Pilot / Flight Attendant, Administrative Assistant, Computer Programmer, Fire Fighter, Bartender, Nurse, Journalist, Photographer, Other?

Skills: *He / she is good at...*

Nouns:

- flower arrangement
- science
- research
- English
- **negotiation**
- navigation
- politics
- computers
- (other)

Gerunds: (verb+ ing)

- cleaning
- making cocktails
- cooking
- listening
- cat-walking
- driving
- communicating
- writing
- (other)

Negotiation (*n.*): a conversation used to find an agreement

B. Lotsa Options

Language Point : Asking About and Expressing Preference

Would rather is used to ask questions and express opinions about preference.

Asking- Would you rather A or B? (*or* for choice)
▸ *Would you rather stay in school or get a job?*

Answering- I would rather A than B. (*than* for comparison)
▸ *I'd rather stay in school than get a job, so I can spend more time with friends.*

◇ Note: The negative form, *I'd rather not,* is a polite way of saying you don't want to do something.
A: *How old are you?*
B: *I'd rather not say.*

Pre-listening

Choose any two of the jobs. Ask your partner which one he/she would rather be and why.
Would you rather be...or...?

a clown

a dolphin trainer

a tailor

a golf ball collector

a tour guide

Listening

 TRACK 16-17

Nick is talking to a career counselor at school about working a summer job. Which job does he decide to apply for?

Tailor's Assistant _____

Party Clown _____

Dolphin Trainer _____

Golf Ball Collector _____

Post-listening

Choose two items from each category.
Ask your partner(s) if they prefer A or B.

Tip: You can also ask about preference using *would you prefer to*.
It has the same meaning.
Would you prefer to live in Paris or Cairo?

1. *Would you rather visit...or...?*

Rome   Cairo   Sydney   San Francisco

2. *Would you rather have...?*

a yacht   a helicopter   an expensive car   a horse and carriage

3. *Would you rather be...?*

famous for your wisdom   famous for your wealth   famous for your beauty   famous for your personality

C. Tinker, Tailor, Soldier, Spy

> Work with a partner to figure out the answers to the tests.
> Then, discuss your results on the final page.

Test 1 Step by Step

Put the words into the boxes in a pattern that makes sense.

Example: Bed   Pillow   Sheet

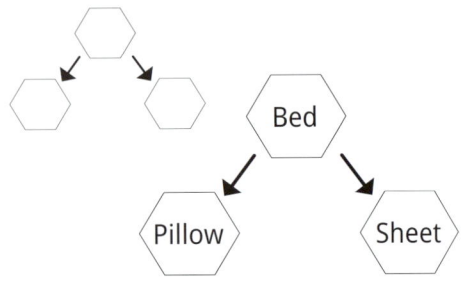

A: *Bed is biggest so it comes first.*
B: *I agree. Pillow and sheet are below bed.*

Branch   Fruit   Leaf   Seed   Juice

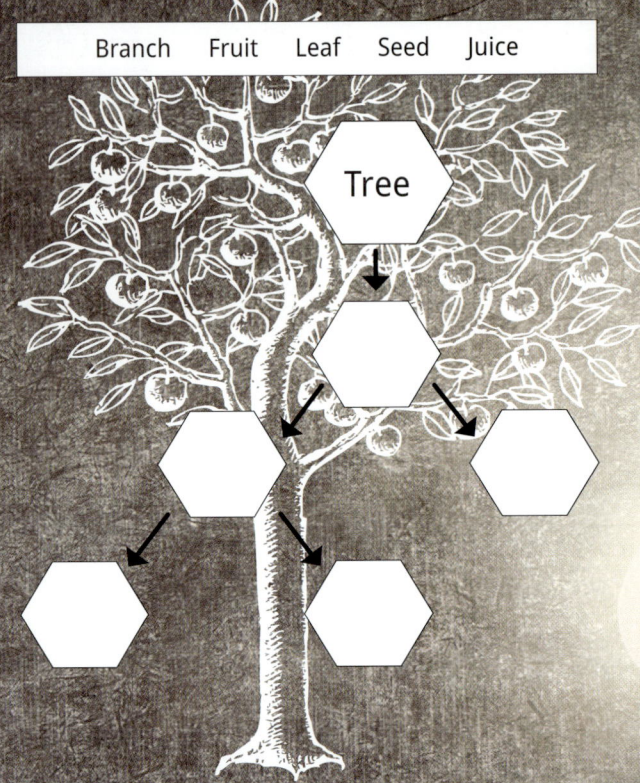

Example: 3   6   9   12   15   _____

A: *Three, six, nine, twelve, fifteen. What do you think the next number in the series is?*
B: *It has to be eighteen because each number increases by three.*

Test 2 Running the Numbers

Ask your partner what he/she thinks the next number in the series is.

1. 6   9   5   8   4   _____
2. 1   3   6   10   15   _____
3. 1   2   4   7   11   _____
4. 16   4   20   24   44   _____

Are you a **number cruncher**? Here's a bonus for you:

6   5   15   10   70   _____

Test 3 Three of a Kind

Give your opinion on which three things are the same in each row.

Example:
A: *Which three things are similar in this row?*
B: *I think the race car, the tram, and the bicycle are similar because they are all forms of transportation.*

 Race car	 Tram	 Key	 Bicycle	 Flower	 Sun Hat

Row 1

 Fish	 Banana	Strawberry	Tent	 Cat	 Lemon

Row 2

Chick	 School Bus	 Conch Shell	 Tractor	 Lobster	Egg

Row 3

 Pineapple	 American Football	Basketball	Globe	 Orange	Anchor

Row 4

 Sneakers	 Saxophone	 Speakers	 Dress Shoes	 Guitar	 Rainbow

Test 4 Opposites Attract

- The square is folded one time. A hole is put in the paper.
- When it is opened, what pattern from below matches the two holes?

Example:
A: *The square is folded once. Then, a hole is put here. What does it look like open?*
B: *I think it matches pattern B.*

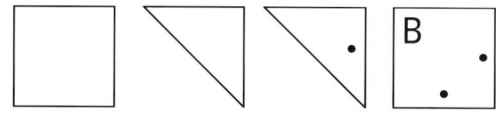

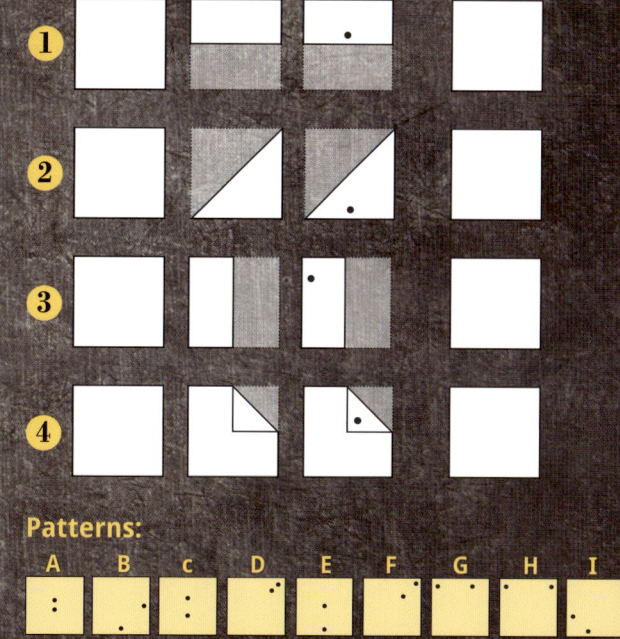

Patterns:
A B C D E F G H I

Number cruncher (n.): a person who works well with numbers and data

Answers:

Test 1: Step by Step

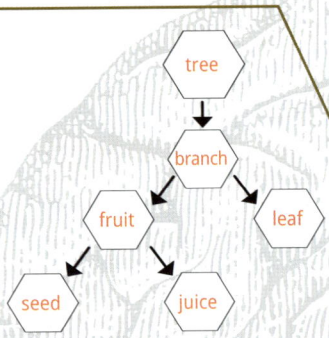

What it measures: The ability to make complicated ideas more easily understood.
Jobs that require this skill: engineer, computer programmer, editor, writer
- Was this test easy or difficult for you?
- Would you like to do one of the jobs above, or would you rather do something else?

Test 2: Running the Numbers

1. 7 (+3-4)
2. 21 (+2+3+4+5+6)
3. 16 (+1+2+3+4+5)
4. 68 (1st + 2nd= 3rd)
Bonus: 61 (-1x3-5x7-9)

What it measures: The ability to understand number patterns.
Jobs that require this skill: economist, financial analyst, accountant
- Was this test easy or difficult for you?
- Would you like to do one of the jobs above, or would you rather do something else?

Test 3: Three of a Kind

Row 1: Banana, Strawberry, Lemon (fruit)
Row 2: Conch, Lobster, Egg (shell)
Row 3: Basketball, Globe, Orange (spheres)
Row 4: Saxophone, Speakers, Guitar (make noise)

Did you see any other things that are related?
What it measures: The ability to analyze and find a pattern in data.
Jobs that require this skill: research scientist, police detective, lawyer
- Was this test easy or difficult for you?
- Would you like to do one of the jobs above, or would you rather do something else?

Test 4: Opposites Attract

1. A   3. H
2. I   4. F

What it measures: The ability to see three-dimensional objects in your mind.
Jobs that require this skill: doctor, architect, designer
- Was this test easy or difficult for you?
- Would you like to do one of the jobs above, or would you rather do something else?

Discussion Questions

1. Would you rather be good at math and bad at English or good at English and bad at math? Why?
   - In reality, which are you better at?

2. Would you rather have a dog or a cat? Why?
   - Would you rather have no pets? Why or why not?

3. Do you think that quizzes such as the last activity are useful for finding what people are good at?
   - Why or why not?
   - What do you think about IQ tests?

4. Would you rather have a lot of experience, or many business contacts? Why?
   - What do you think of people that get hired to work at companies because of who they know?

5. What would be the perfect job for you?
   - Where would the job be located?
   - How many hours a day would you work?
   - How much would you get paid?
   - Do you think you'll ever have this job? Why or why not?

6. What do you think about having to work on weekends?
   - Would you rather work ten hours a day for four days or eight hours a day for five days?
   - Should companies be forced to pay extra money to employees that work more than forty hours a week?

LESSON 2

>> WARM UP

Objectives:
/ Discuss lengths of time
/ Practice interviewing for a job

1. 100 years ago, the jobs in these pictures were common. How about now?

2. What other jobs can you think of that people don't do anymore?

3. In your opinion, what are some of the most important jobs today? Why do you think so?

Blacksmith

Switchboard Operator

Milkman

152 | SLE Generations 1C

A. Long, Long Time

Language Point: *For* and *From / To* With the Simple Past

Use *for* to describe a length of time. (several weeks, a couple of days, a long time)
▶ *I worked there for a few hours, but they fired me.*

Use *from/to* to describe a start and end time. (yesterday to today, middle school to high school)
▶ *I worked from 8 a.m. to 9 p.m. yesterday.*

PART 1 ● From Here to Eternity

1. How long was your last vacation?
   • From when to when?
2. How long did you work / attend school yesterday?
   • From when to when?
3. How long did it take you to get to class today?
   • From when to when?
4. How long did you work at your first part-time job?
   • From when to when?
5. How long did you sleep last night?
   • From when to when?

Language Point: *For* and *Since* With the Present Perfect

Use *for* to describe a <u>length</u> of time. (a **decade**, two hours, five minutes)
▶ *He has worked here for eighteen years.*

Use *since* to describe a specific starting time (June, 2008, the day we met):
▶ *He has worked here since graduation.*

PART 2 ● Since Forever

Ask your partner the question. Answer your partner using *for*. Then switch. Ask your partner the same question. Answer your partner using *since*.

How long have you...
1. been in class?
2. had your current hairstyle?
3. owned your current phone?
4. lived in your present home?
5. worked at your job / attended your school?

Decade (*n.*): period of ten years

B. Get Back to Work!

Practice these interview questions with a partner.
> Ask the follow-up questions for more information.
> Try to think of additional questions to keep the conversation interesting.
> Tip: You can tell the truth, but you don't have to! You can make up whatever you want.

Interview Questions Student A	Yes / No	Follow-up Questions — Extra Info
Can you . . .		
speak another language?		How long have you studied it?
Are you . . .		
hardworking?		Can you give me an example?
Are you good at . . .		
solving work problems?		Tell me about a problem you helped solve.
giving presentations?		
Are you able to . . .		
meet **deadlines**?		What have you done to meet deadlines?
Do you know how to . . .		
use Microsoft Excel?		How long have you used it?
communicate effectively?		
Do you have . . .		
any previous work experience?		How long did you work there?
Have you ever...		
lived or worked overseas?		How long were you there?
Do you have experience...		
handling money?		
developing projects?		How long did your last project take?

Interview Questions Student B	Yes / No	Follow-up Questions — Extra Info
Can you . . .		
use Power Point?		
speak another language?		How long have you studied it?
Are you . . .		
organized?		Can you give me an example?
Are you good at . . .		
writing emails?		
Are you able to . . .		
work **under pressure**?		Tell me about a stressful situation you handled well.
Do you know how to . . .		
use Microsoft Excel?		How long have you used it?
Do you have . . .		
any experience?		How long did you work at your last job?
any degrees?		
Have you ever...		
had a disagreement with a boss or coworker?		How did you solve the problem?
lived or worked overseas?		How long were you there?
Do you have experience...		
leading people?		

Deadline (*n.*): the time set to finish a project
Under pressure (*idiom*): feeling stressed to finish something

C. Tic Tac Toad

> To take a square, complete the sentence.
> Make a true statement about yourself.
> Remember your partner's information.

I've been cute since I was born!

Round 1

I'd rather eat...than...	...for five years.	I'd rather go to...than...
...for one hour.	I'd rather work with...than...	...since I was born.
I'd rather see a...movie than a...movie	...since middle school.	I'd rather drink...than...

Round 2

I'd rather live in...than...	...since 2012.	...for just a short time.
I'd rather play...than...	...since last October.	I'd rather spend my time ...~ing than ...~ing.
...for three days.	I'd rather visit...than...	...for a long time.

Unit 8 Occupational Hazard | 155

Bonus round:

> This time, report what you remember about your partner.
> You need 4 in a row to win this round.

...for just a short time.	You would rather spend your time ...~ing than ...~ing.	...for a long time.	...since 2012.
...since last October.	You would rather visit ...than...	...since middle school.	You'd rather play...than...
...for three days.	You'd rather eat...than...	You would rather go to... than...	...since you were born.
You'd rather work with... than...	You would rather drink ...than...	You'd rather see a ...movie than a...	...for five years.

Discussion Questions

1. How long have cell phones been common?
   - Do you think you could live without a cell phone now?
   - How would your life be different?

2. In your opinion, is it alright to lie in a job interview?
   - What about **exaggerating** on your **résumé**?
   - What about changing your résumé photo?

3. Do you think that internships are useful for learning career skills? Why or why not?
   - What about part-time jobs?
   - What other activities are good for learning career skills?

4. In your country, how important is it to be **punctual**?
   - Is it acceptable to be five or ten minutes late for a business meeting?

5. Would you rather work eight hours a day at a boring job or work twelve hours a day at a really interesting job? Why?

6. Would you rather work with a nice boss and mean coworkers or a **mean** boss and nice coworkers? Why?

UNIT 8 REVIEW

How well can you use…
- ☐ "Would rather" to express preference?
- ☐ Ways to discuss lengths of time?

What do you need to study more?

Exaggerate *(v.)*: describe something as more than the reality
Résumé *(n.)*: a summary of skills and education
Punctual *(adj.)*: on time; not late
Mean *(adj.)*: unkind

Activity: Hiring Manager

- You and your partner are hiring managers.
- Discuss who you would rather hire for the job.
- Give as many reasons as possible.

Example: Salesperson

A: *I would rather hire Andrew because I think soccer players have a lot of discipline.*

Andrew

He has looked for a job since graduating earlier this year.

He did an internship at an insurance company from graduation to last month.

He played soccer for four years in college.

He was student president of his university for two years.

1. Job: Salesperson

Gina

She worked as a salesperson for five years.

She was the top salesperson for the first two years.

She has not worked since having a baby.

She graduated at the top of her college class.

She went to university from age eighteen to age twenty eight.

Brutus

He has worked as a security guard for eighteen years.

He has tried to improve his manners since last year because some customers said they were scared of him.

He went to university for two years but got kicked out.

▶ Which candidate has more experience?

▶ Which candidate has better education?

▶ Which candidate's life experience is more useful?

2. Job: Security Guard

Imagine that you are applying for these jobs.

- What skills and experience would you mention?
- Which job would you rather do?

Carla

She has worked as a barista in a café for the last two years.

She studied child psychology for four years in college.

She has never worked as a security guard.

She studied martial arts from age ten to age twenty.

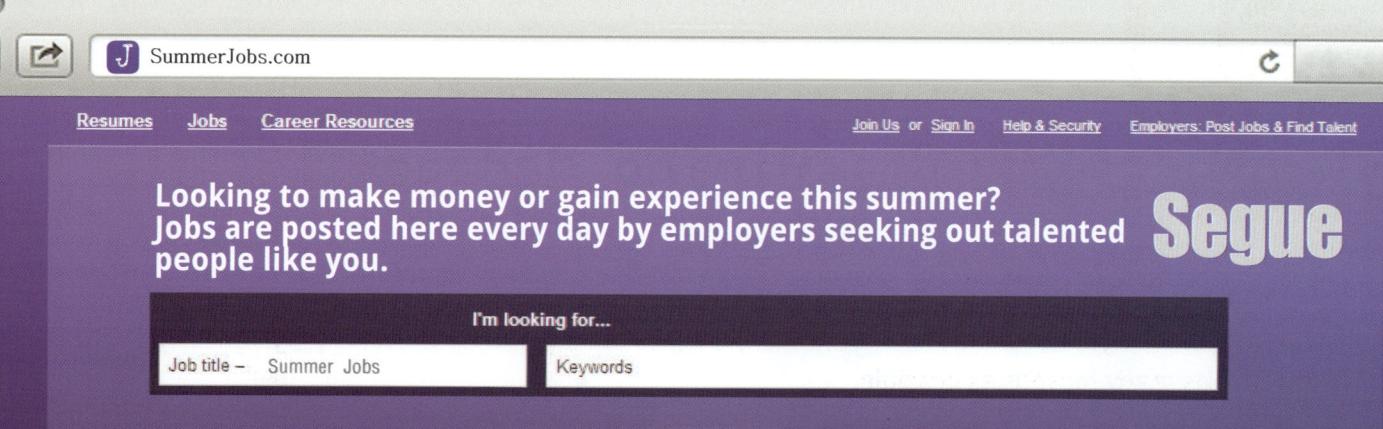

Job: Tailor's Assistant
Location: Tod's Tuxes and Custom Suits
Description: Helping a master tailor to measure customers for custom suits and wedding tuxedos. We have a lot of work to do getting people fitted in wedding attire. We are located downtown in the business district.
Pay: $15/hr.
Hours: 4 days a week. 9-6

Job: Clown
Location: Big Fun Day Camp
Description: Playing games and entertaining kids at a summer day camp. You will sing songs, lead activities, and tell jokes for 5-10 year old kids. Located just out of town, next to a big park.
Pay: $12/hr.
Hours: Monday-Friday. 9-3.

Job: Dolphin Trainer
Location: City Aquarium
Description: Help the marine biologists at the aquarium with the feeding and care of the dolphins. You should love being around animals and getting wet.
Pay: Internship
Hours: Tuesday-Sunday. 8-4.

Job: Tour Guide
Location: Downtown Tours
Description: Take tourists on free tours of the historic downtown area. Plenty of walking and talking are involved. You should enjoy meeting different people from all over the world.
Pay: $10/hr.
Hours: Thursday-Sunday. 10-5.

Job: Golf Ball Collector
Location: County Golf Course
Description: Driving around the machine that picks up the golf balls on the driving range. You should have strong nerves as many golfers will see you as a target. But don't worry, the machine is protected by a cage.
Pay: $11/hr.
Hours: Any three days a week you want. 8-8.

A. Discussion
1. Have you ever had a part-time or summer job?
   - What did you do at the job?
   - What were the best and worst parts of the job?
2. Would you like to do any of the jobs above? Why or why not?

B. Writing
Write a job description like the ones above for a summer job you would like to do.
- What is the job?
- Where is it located?
- What do you do at this job?
- How much does it pay, and what are the hours?

09
Once Upon A Time
Morals & Anecdotes

Objectives:
/ Practice telling anecdotes and stories
/ Listen to an anecdote about a night out

WARM UP

1. Who is the best story teller in your family?
   - What makes his/her stories interesting?

2. Would you rather hear a funny story or a dramatic story?
   - Why?

3. What was your favorite story when you were young?
   - Would children enjoy this story today?

4. Where is the best place to hear stories now?

LESSON 1

A. Up On a Time

Language Point : Telling a Story in Sequence

- At the beginning of stories or instructions, use expressions like:
  First,... To begin (with),... First of all,...

- To sequence the events, use a mix of expressions like:
  Then,... Next,... After that,... Later,...

- End stories with expressions like:
  Finally,... In the end,...

◇Note: You can use "Then," "Next," and "After that," in any order. Mix them for variety.

PART 1 • With a partner, put the story below in order. Take turns choosing a sequence word and matching it to the part of the story that comes next.

1. First of all,	A. ...the police said to leave the area.
2. Then,	B. ...people came back and repaired the damage.
3. After that,	C. ...the rain stopped.
4. Then,	D. ...the rain came.
5. Next,	E. ...things were back to normal.
6. After that,	F. ...people went to stay in other places.
7. Finally,	G. ...the water rose while the people slept.

1. Once upon a time, there was a town that had a big flood.

162 | SLE Generations 1C

PART 2 • With a partner, fill in the missing details about Jack and Jill's story in your own words.

1. To begin with, Jack and his friend Nick...
2. After they went in, Jack saw Jill...
3. He asked her...
4. Later that week, Jack...
5. Then, they...
6. Next, they...
7. Some time went by, and...
8. And after that,...
9. A few months later,...
10. Then,...
11. But next,...
In the end,...

Share your story with another group.
- How are the stories different?
- In what ways are they similar?

Unit 9 Once Upon A Time | 163

B. One Wild Night

Language Point : Telling Anecdotes

Telling an anecdote is easy and an important part of conversations.
Just follow these steps:

1. Create interest with an **opening**:
- There was this one time when…
- I'll never forget the time…

I'll never forget the day I met your mother.

2. Tell the **story** in sequence:
- First,…
- So,… Then,… Next,…
- Finally,…

3. Explain the point of the story:
- So that's why…
- After, I realized…

So that's why you should always talk to people at the bus stop.

Did You know?

- An **anecdote** is a short story about a true event. The story is often told to make a point about an experience.

Pre-listening

Match the parts of an anecdote on the left with their definitions on the right.

1. An introduction
2. The beginning
3. The main story
4. The ending
5. The purpose

A gives the events in order.

B explains how the story started.

C says why the story is important.

D gives the background and explains why it is interesting.

E tells the listener what finally happened.

Listening  TRACK 18-19

Ella is about to go out for the night, and her brother Nick gives her some advice.
Listen, and check the dishes Nick's friend actually eats in the story.

Post-listening

Language Point : Active Listening

When someone is telling a story, the person listening shows interest by repeating part of what she is hearing and asking for more information.

1. **Mirroring**
A: *Then, I went outside for awhile.*
B: *Okay, you went outside. Then what happened?*

2. **Asking for more information**
A: *There was a strange guy outside.*
B: *Why did you think he was strange?*
A: *He was wearing a watermelon helmet!*

Tell an anecdote about a time you went out with friends or family. Use the answers to these questions to guide your story.

1. How old were you?
2. Who did you go out with?
3. What was the occasion? (Why did you go out?)
4. What was your plan?
5. What happened first?
6. What happened next?
7. What did you do after that?
8. What happened in the end?
9. What did you learn from the experience?

C. Anecdotal Evidence

Practice telling anecdotes and asking questions with a partner or group.

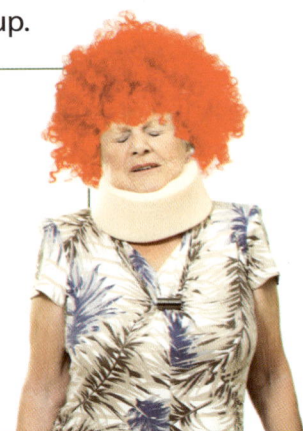

Example: Riding the subway

A: *I was on the subway one day when something surprising happened.*
B: *What happened?*
A: *First, an old lady sat down next to me.*
B: *What was she doing?*
A: *She was wearing a bright orange wig and a neck brace.*
B: *Oh wow. A wig and neck brace? Alright, what happened after she sat down?*
A: *Well, then she……*

PART 1

Story Teller: Tell your partner a story from your life.
Possible starters:
A. I was riding the subway this one day when…
B. I was relaxing at home this one time, and…
C. One night, I was sleeping when something happened…
D. Once I was visiting my relatives, and…

Listener: Ask as many questions as possible.
Possible questions:
A. Which subway line were you riding?
   Were you standing or sitting?
B. You were relaxing at home? What were you doing?
C. You were sleeping? What time was it?
D. Where do your relatives live?
   How big is your family?

PART 2 • Try telling anecdotes about these topics:

- A time something went wrong
- A time you discovered a new interest
- A time you got something valuable for free
- A time you wanted to hide
- A time you made a new friend
- A time you lied to your parents
- A mistake you made

Discussion Questions

1. In your opinion, where is the best place to meet new people?
   - ▶ Can you easily talk to strangers in public places? Why or why not?

2. Have you ever gotten into an argument with a friend during a trip or vacation?
   - ▶ What happened?

3. Do you have a friend or family member that tells the same stories over and over?
   - ▶ If yes, what are the stories about?
   - ▶ If not, what stories do you enjoy hearing over and over?

4. What is an interesting story about something that is happening now?
   - ▶ What is the best way to find out about current events?

5. Has a friend ever told you an unbelievable story?
   - ▶ What happened?

6. Who is your favorite actor, athlete, or famous person?
   - ▶ What interesting story have you heard about this person?

LESSON 2

>> WARM UP

Objectives:
/ Review reported speech
/ Discuss morals of stories

Using the pictures below to answer the following questions.
What important lesson should all children learn?
Why do you think this lesson is important?

Cooperation

Diligence

Kindness

Respect

Patience

Cleanliness

A. Fabled Speech

Language Point : Reported Speech Review

Changing the verb being reported to past forms:

Statements	What did he say?
"I know," he said.	He said that he <u>knew</u>.
Yes / No questions	What did he ask?
"Do you know her?" he asked.	He asked if I <u>knew</u> her.
Information questions	What did he ask?
"What do you know?" he asked.	He asked what I <u>knew</u>.

◇Note: 1. In spoken English, it is common for people to not change the verb to the past when the event being reported just happened.

2. The pronouns change to the reporter's point of view.
   Romeo said, "I love you, Juliet."
   Correct: *Romeo said <u>he</u> loved <u>her</u>.*
   Incorrect: *Romeo said I loved you.*

PART 1 • Change the following to reported speech in the same way:

The Princess and the Frog

A: *What did the princess say?*
B: *She asked the frog if* _____
A: *What did the frog say?*
B: *He said* _____

Cinderella

What did the prince ask?

How did Cinderella answer?

What did she ask him?

PART 2 • Winter's Coming

With a partner, complete the story by filling in the missing pieces.

A. "Winter is coming."
The ant said winter was coming.

A. "You need to work hard."
The ant said _____ needed to work hard.

A. "Do you have enough food for later?"
The ant asked the grasshopper _____ _____ had enough food for later.

A. "What will you eat in the winter?"
The ant asked _____ _____ _____ eat in the winter.

B. "I'm not worried."
The grasshopper said he wasn't worried.

B. "I'd rather enjoy myself!"
The grasshopper said _____ would rather enjoy _____.

B. "Are you crazy?"
The grasshopper asked the ant _____ _____ _____ crazy.

B. "Why do you worry so much?"
The grasshopper asked _____ _____ _____ so much.

Continue reporting the dialogue using the same patterns.

A. "Why is it so cold?"
The grasshopper asked...

A. "Can you give me some food?"
The grasshopper asked...

A. "I need your help."
The grasshopper said...

B. "It's winter."
The ant said...

B. "Do you remember my warning last summer?"
The ant asked _____ _____ _____ his warning last summer.

B. "Why should I help you?"
The ant asked...

What happened next? Finish the story.

B. Lesson Learned

> Take turns telling these **fables** with a partner.
> At the end of the story, choose the correct moral.

The Tortoise and the Hare:

Once upon a time, there was...
One day, the hare asked the tortoise...
The tortoise said...
Then,...
Next,...
After that,...
Finally,...

What's the **moral of the story**?
A. Don't skip your nap, or you'll be in a bad mood.
B. Slow and steady wins the race.
C. A tortoise is not a turtle.

The Boy Who Cried Wolf:

Once upon a time, there was a shepherd boy who always...
One day, the boy decided to trick the villagers, so he cried...
The villagers came, and they asked the boy...
The boy laughed and said...
After that,...
The boy screamed...
The villagers heard him, but...

What's the moral of the story?
A. Don't fall in love with a wolf.
B. Don't lose people's trust, or they won't believe you when you tell the truth.
C. Taking care of sheep is really boring.

The Lion and the Mouse:

| Once upon a time, there was... |
| One day,... |
| Then, the mouse asked the lion... |
| Later, the lion... |
| He asked the mouse... |
| In the end,... |
| What is the moral of the story?
A. Be kind to everybody even if they are weak. You don't know who might help you in the future.
B. Never ask a lion if he is hungry, or he might eat you.
C. If you're large, watch out for traps! |

The Frog and The Scorpion:

| Once upon a time,... |
| One day, the scorpion said... |
| The frog was worried. He asked... |
| The scorpion said... |
| Then,... |
| After that,... |
| Finally,... |
| What is the moral of the story?
A. Scorpions are not cool.
B. Don't expect people to change their character.
C. Frogs are weak. |

Fable (*n.*): a traditional story, usually with animal characters and a moral
Moral of the story (*n.*): lesson taught by the story

C. The Animal and The Animal

Create a fable with animals, reported conversations, and a lesson.

1. What value(s) will this fable teach?
   Choose one with a partner.

Example:
A: *Let's make a fable to teach kids about courage.*
B: *Okay, kids need to be brave.*

Planning   Kindness
Teamwork   Courage
Studiousness   Ambition
Honesty   Politeness
Respect   (other)

2. Choose two animals for your main characters.
   Give each one two personality traits.

Animal #1:
Positive trait:
Negative trait:

Animal #2:
Positive trait:
Negative trait:

Positive
A. Energetic
B. Outgoing
C. Dependable
D. Calm
E. Brave
F. Clever
G. Creative
H. Determined
I. **Ambitious**
J. Loyal

Negative
K. Sensitive
L. Arrogant
M. Mean
N. Careless
O. **Impulsive**
P. Judgmental
Q. Shy
R. Cowardly
S. Lazy
T. Impatient

 Rat    Ox    Tiger    Hare    Dragon   Snake

 Horse    Ram    Monkey    Rooster    Dog    Pig

3. Where will this story take place?

| In a forest | In the ocean | In a desert |
| On a mountain | In a jungle | (other) |

Ambitious (*adj.*): having a strong desire to be successful
Impulsive (*adj.*): acting without thinking

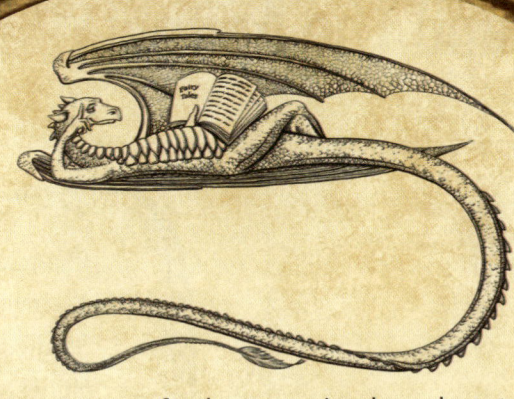

4. Now, make an opening statement for the story using these characters and the location.
Once upon a time, there was…
Your story _____

5. Create the opening scene.
One day,…
Your story _____

6. Explain very simply what happened between the opening scene and the ending.
Next,… / After that,… / Then,…
Your story _____

7. Tell how the story ends.
Finally,…
Your story _____

8. What is the moral of the story?

> **Example:** *The moral of the story is be brave because you never know what might happen.*
>
> Useful patterns for morals of stories:
> Don't _____ unless _____.
> **Example:** *Don't be selfish unless you want people to ignore you when you need help.*
>
> Always _____. It doesn't matter if _____.
> **Example:** *Always be kind. It doesn't matter if you think somebody is weaker than you.*
>
> Never _____, or _____.
> **Example:** *Never give up on your dreams, or you will regret it later in life.*

9. (optional) Present your story to the class.

Discussion Questions

1. Do you think that fables are a good way to teach values to children? Why or why not?
   - ▶ What fable or story did you like to hear when you were younger?

2. Would you rather be friends with a person who is loyal but bad-tempered or a person who is friendly but dishonest? Why?
   - ▶ What are your best qualities?
   - ▶ What are your worst qualities?

3. What movies do you think teach a good story or lesson?

4. What story from history do you think is important for all people to know?

5. What is your favorite book?
   - ▶ Who is the author?
   - ▶ What is the story about?

6. What popular stories do you think teach people a bad message?

UNIT 9 REVIEW

How well can you use…
- ☐ Sequencing for telling anecdotes?
- ☐ Ways to report what others have said or asked?

What do you need to study more?

Activity: Animal Proverbs

PART 1 ● With a partner, replace the highlighted part of the sentence with one of the proverbs.

A. The early bird catches the worm.	B. You can't teach an old dog new tricks.	C. Don't count your chicks before they hatch.	D. When the cat is away the mouse will play.	E. Never look a gift horse in the mouth.
F. There is more than one way to skin a cat.	G. If it looks like a duck and quacks like a duck, it's a duck.	H. Birds of a feather flock together.	I. You can lead a horse to water, but you can't make it drink.	J. There are other fish in the sea.

1. When she went overseas to study she just spent time with people from her own country. **People like to spend time with others who are similar.**

2. She gave you those shoes for free, and you said to her that you don't like the color. **If someone offers you a gift, don't question it.**

3. You're not sure if you got the promotion, but you bought a new car! **Don't start making decisions until you are sure you have succeeded.**

4. I told her to break up with him, but she didn't listen. Now he's cheated on her. **You can try to help someone, but you can't force them to accept your advice.**

5. She got to the sale right before they opened and was able to get a huge discount. **You need to be early if you want to succeed.**

6. Grandpa has so much trouble learning how to use his smart phone. **It's hard for people to learn something new the older they get.**

7. When the boss went on vacation, everyone just surfed the Internet and chatted. **When someone isn't there to watch, people will just do what they want.**

8. I know you're really sad because she broke up with you, but don't worry. **There are a lot more people out there.**

9. If we can't get there by bus, we could always take the train. **There is more than one way to do something.**

10. The fast food restaurant says it is selling *healthy burgers*. I don't know. **If it looks like what it is, how can it be different?**

PART 2 ● Think of a proverb that is used in your language. Try to translate it into English, and explain it to the class.

Harry: I went out for a burger with Nick last night. We got lost and ended up in Mexico! I didn't have my passport, so Nick had to drive back and get it.
This is my new friend, Choi. He was hanging out by the taco shop.

Segue

Things Went South!

 Jane: Cool! A zebra. What did you guys do together?

 Harry: I tried to take him to a seafood place, but he didn't like it. Zebras are vegetarians apparently.

 Bobby: That's not a zebra. That's a donkey with black lines painted on it. What happened next?

 Harry: Choi started stomping his foot. He wanted to go to an ice cream place! We ate about ten ice cream cones. After that, he ran away. I was so full I fell asleep at the table. Finally, Nick found me, and we went home.

 Jane: I guess the moral of the story is: don't hang out with zebra-donkeys in Mexico!

A. Discussion

1. Have you ever had a difficult experience while travelling?
   - What did you learn from this experience?
2. How often do you go out to eat?
   - What kind of restaurants do you enjoy going out to?

B. Writing

Write a short paragraph detailing a night you went out and ate well.
- Where did you go?
- Who were you with?
- What did you eat and drink there?
- Why would you recommend it?

WARM UP

SELF EVALUATION:
Look at the list of topics and skills we studied.
Which topics and skills did you improve? = √
Which skills do you need to study more? = O
Which skills do you not know? = X

Unit 1 Been There, Done That
☐ Using *It* as the subject   √ O X
☐ Asking questions about experience   √ O X

Unit 2 Tailor Made
☐ Asking for favors and permission   √ O X
☐ Describing where and how things are made   √ O X

Unit 3 Look Before You Leap
☐ Giving warnings and showing prohibition   √ O X
☐ Comparing prohibition to necessity   √ O X

Unit 4 It Takes All Kinds!
☐ Giving impressions   √ O X
☐ Using –ing adjectives to describe situations   √ O X

Unit 5 X Marks The Spot
☐ Reporting questions   √ O X
☐ Talking about similarities and differences   √ O X

Unit 6 I'm Glad You Asked
☐ Describing location and giving directions   √ O X
☐ Giving directions on public transportation   √ O X

Unit 7 I'm Glad You Asked
☐ Talking about existence   √ O X
☐ Degrees of certainty   √ O X

Unit 8 Occupational Hazard
☐ Expressing preference with *would rather*   √ O X
☐ Expressing lengths of time   √ O X

Unit 9 Once Upon A Time
☐ Sequencing stories   √ O X
☐ Using reported speech   √ O X

Evaluation	
√ = 3 points	**42-54 points:** Ready for the next level, 2A.
O = 2 points	**30-42 points:** Maybe stay in 1C one more month to improve.
X = 1 point	**18-30 points:** Need to study 1C again.

Unit 10 Looking Back | 179

LESSON 1

A. Porkus Lupus

Match each number to a picture, and finish the sentence. Then, tell the story in order.
Ask your partner as many extra questions as you can while telling the story.

1. A: *What letter starts the story?* B: *A. Once upon a time there were three pigs.* A: *What were their names?* B: *Their names were...*	2. A: *What happened in the end?* B: *Finally,...*
3. A: *What did the first pig do?* B: *He made...*	4. A: *What did the second pig do?* B: *He...*
5. A: *What did the third pig do?* B: *He...*	6. A: *Who else was there?* B: *There was a _____*
7. A: *What did the pigs decide to do?* B: *They...*	8. A: *What did the wolf say to the first pig?*
9. A: *What did the wolf say to the second pig?*	10. A: *What did the wolf say to the third pig?*

B. Take It Easy

Pre-listening

Discuss with a partner how each of the family members is getting to their destination and what he / she might be doing once they get there.

Example: Bobby
A: *Where is Bobby going, and how is he getting there?*
B: *He's taking an elephant, and he might be…*

Listening TRACK 20-21

Check your answers while listening to the family's plans for the summer.

Bobby

Henry

David

Nick

Ella

Ruth

Heather

Unit 10 Looking Back | 181

Post-listening

Practice asking and answering the questions about a place you would like to travel to. If you can't think of anywhere you would like to go, use the fact sheet for Switzerland to answer the questions.

1. Where would you like to go on your next trip?
2. Where is _____ ?
3. Who do you want to go with?
4. What transportation can you take to get there?
5. Have you been there before?
6. Why do you want to visit _____ ?
7. How long do you want to go for?
8. Are there any famous sites to see?
9. What activities are there to enjoy there?
   (museums, shopping, sports, etc.)
10. What transportation do you need to take to get around?
11. What kind of accommodation would you stay in?
    (hotel, guesthouse, hostel, camping, etc.)
12. What kind of food can you enjoy there?
13. What kind of souvenir will you look for?
14. What things do you have to be careful of while there?
    (crime, natural disasters, etc.)

MATTERHORN

SWITZERLAND

Country Profile: Switzerland

Capital: Bern
Other cities: Zurich, Geneva, Basel
Languages: German, French, Italian
Currency: Swiss Franc
Food and Drink: Beer, Wine, Bread, Cheese, Chocolate, Muesli, Sausages
Natural Places: Swiss National Park, Matterhorn Mountain, The Rhine Falls, St. Moritz ski area
Cultural Attractions: Geneva Fountain (world's tallest), Basel spring carnival, Chillon Castle, St. Gallen medieval city
Shopping: Cow Bells, Cuckoo Clocks, Watches, Chocolate
Getting Around- Trains, Bicycles, Lake Steamers (boats)

C. Comedy of Errors

- Divide into teams.
- Flip a coin to decide which team gets the square.
- If your team wins the coin toss, correct the sentence.
- A correct answer is worth two points.
- Flip a coin to move forward. The team with the most points at the end of the game wins!

START	It is cold outside?	Who's name did you said it was?	Did you ever went to Spain?	Yes, I haven't.	I don't liking chocolate.
If it is raining outside, you takes an umbrella.	These shoes are made for leather.	I play swimming.	She likes going tennis.	May you help me with something?	Can I has one? -Of course you can't
How much apples is there?	You would better study hard.	There are books in the table.	There is students on the room.	I am boring in class today.	He is a very interested person.
He must sick. He usually comes.	I have a vacation starting in Monday.	I like chocolate. -So am I.	She are eating a hamburger.	The teacher ask when my weekend was.	Can you holding your breath for one minute?
I'd rather to stay at home than to see a movie.	I have studied English since five years.	That's him phone.	He say to told him my name.	It's maybe will snow.	FINISH

D. Tit for Tat

> **Example:**
>
> **A:** *Could you add surfing lessons?*
> **B:** *Yes, that's fine. I'll give you unlimited surfing for the year. Can you add a starlight headliner to my car?*
> **A:** *No problem. Now, do you plan to cook for yourself?*
> **B:** *Hmm. Not really. Could you arrange for meals?*
> **A:** *We have a really great chef, but he's a little expensive.*
> **B:** *Could you trade a year of meals for something?*

STUDENT A

> You own a car dealership, but you need a vacation.
> You want to trade some of your cars for a year of accommodations on an island.
> You get to keep the things you don't trade.
> Negotiate the exchange.

Sports car: $70,000   **Sedan:** $30,000   **Golf Cart:** $4,000   **Buggy:** $3000 **Horse:** $5000

Air-conditioned massaging seats   **Rear-seat beverage cooler**   **Underwater Capability**

$15,000

$1500 for the cooler
$5000 for a year of soda and beer refills

$30,000

Passenger entertainment system   **Passenger mannequins**   **Starlight headliner on ceiling**

$2,000

$4,000 for celebrity mannequin
$6,000 for a mannequin of yourself

$5,000

STUDENT B

> You are the owner of a gorgeous island in the South Pacific.
> You want to trade one year of accommodations at a vacation house on your island for a car.
> You get to keep the rest.
> Negotiate the exchange.

$100,000 for a year

$45,000 for a year

$6,000 for a year

Gourmet meal delivery		$40 for a meal, prepaid -OR- $30,000 for one full year (3 meals a day)	Indoor dolphin tank		$15,000 a year for the tank with one dolphin Extra dolphins $5,000 for each year
Saturday beach party with food and music		$50 for one party, prepaid -OR- $1,500 for forty parties	Surfing lessons and equipment		$50 for one hour, prepaid -OR- $3,000 for unlimited access
Gardening and landscaping service		$7,000 for the year	Daily housekeeping service		$5,000 for the year

Example:

A: *Could you add surfing lessons?*
B: *Yes, that's fine. I'll give you unlimited surfing for the year. Can you add a starlight headliner to my car?*
A: *No problem. Now, do you plan to cook for yourself?*
B: *Hmm. Not really. Could you arrange for meals?*
A: *We have a really great chef, but he's a little expensive.*
B: *Could you trade a year of meals for something?*

E. Haunted House

- Your friends dared you to spend the night in a famous haunted house.
- Follow the directions to see what happens. You will need a coin.
- You have 4 lives.

Another friendly ghost appears and offers you more stuff. **Choose three more items.**

 a. Monster Swatter  b. Medicine

 c. Toilet paper  d. Night Light

 e. Life Jacket  f. Fire Suit

Step 1: You're going into the house...

Tails

Go down to the basement.

Killer Clown ties you up. You lose one life unless you have the magic lotion. Do you?

Heads

Go up the staircase.

All is well. Go to the next step.

A friendly ghost appears and offers you supplies. **Choose two.**

Example: *I'll take the pizza because I love pizza and the toothbrush because brushing your teeth is important.*

Magic Lotion

Toothbrush

Camera

Pizza

Step 3: Flip a coin.

Heads

Go in through the front door.

You lose one life unless you can cure the vampire's toothache with the toothbrush. Can you?

Tails

Go in through the window.

You have to give some food to Captain Kill. Did you bring something? If not, lose one life.

Step 2: Flip a coin.

Step 5: Flip a coin.

Heads
Enter the sauna.
This sauna is too hot. Lose one life unless you have a fire suit. Do you? Go to Step 7.

Tails
Enter the ballroom.
The Woman in Red asks a question. You have to be careful how you answer. Go to the next step.

Heads
Go into the bedroom and take a nap for an hour.
You'd better have a monster swatter. Do you? If not, lose one life.

Tails
Hang out with the Gingerbread Monster and have a snack.
Enjoy your food! Gain one extra life! Go to the next step.

Step 6: Flip a coin.

Heads
Tell the Woman in Red she's pretty.
She's happy. All is well. Go to the next step.

Tails
Tell the Woman in Red she needs to go on a diet.
She turns into a werewolf. Lose one life.

Step 9: Flip a coin.

Heads
Eat the mushrooms on the table.
These are deadly poisonous mushrooms. Lose one life unless you have medicine. Do you?

Tails
Drink the water.
If you drink the water, you get sick. Lose one life unless you have the toilet paper.

Step 8: Flip a coin.

Step 7: Flip a coin.

Heads
Go into the kitchen.
Would you like a glass of water or some delicious mushrooms? Go to the next step.

Tails
Go into the bathroom.
You'd better have a life jacket. Do you? No? Lose one life. Go to the kitchen.

Unit 10 Looking Back | 187

Who finished with the most lives?
You are truly a survivor.

END.

Step 10:

Another friendly ghost appears. **Choose two more items.**

a. Tunnel

b. Parachute

c. Diving Suit

d. Salad Dressing

Heads

Tell your friends what happened.

Your friends won't believe you unless you took pictures.
If you have the camera, gain one life.

Tails

Keep it a secret.

Killer Clown will visit you every night in your dreams. Lose one life, unless you have the night light.

Step 11: Flip a coin.

Heads

Go down the stairs to leave.

The killer plant gets you, and you lose one life unless you put salad dressing on it.
Can you?

Tails

Jump out the window to leave.

You'd better have a parachute, or you fall and break a fingernail. Do you have one?
If not, lose one more life.

Step 13: Flip a coin.

Heads

Run away through the cornfield.

You get lost. Lose one life unless you have a tunnel. Do you?

Tails

Swim away across the river.

There are piranhas.! You need a diving suit to protect you. Do you have one? If not, lose a life.

Step 12: Flip a coin.

188 | SLE Generations 1C

F. Review Discussion

First, ask a question about the family. Use the listening scripts in the back of the book to help you answer. Then, ask a question about what you learned.

1. What is Grandpa Henry trying to learn?
2. Have you ever tried to write code? When? If not, do you want to?

3. How much did Heather pay Nick for the cup of coffee? Why that much?
4. What things are made in your country? How often do you buy these products?

5. What does Grandpa Henry tell Bobby to not do in the cave?
6. What is something you can't do if there is a fire?

7. How did Jack seem to Ella during their date?
8. What is the most exciting thing that has happened to you recently?

UNIT 5
9. What is something the reporter asked David about his former student?
10. What is something you and another person in the class both like?

11. Grandpa Henry is trying to get from where to where when he calls Nick?
12. How do I get to your house from here using public transportation?

13. What strange ingredient is there in Grandma Ruth's lasagna?
14. What is something that might happen in your life soon?

15. What summer job does Nick decide to apply for?
16. How long have you lived in your current house / apartment?

17. What does Nick tell Ella to bring with her on her night out?
18. What important lesson did you learn as child?

2A
19. Do you know what indirect questions are?
20. You're going to study next month in 2A, aren't you?

Activity: Dogball

1. How many players are there on each team?
2. How long is the game?
3. How many dogs are on the court during the game? What else is there on the court?
4. How big is the ball, and what material is it made of? (leather, steel, cookies)
5. How do you score points in this game?
6. What happens if a dog gets the ball?
7. What equipment do the players get? (rackets, gloves, horses, swords)

Create a new sport called Dogball.
It is played on a stone court with rings high on the wall.
There are dogs running around on the court.
Decide the other details, and present your game to the class.

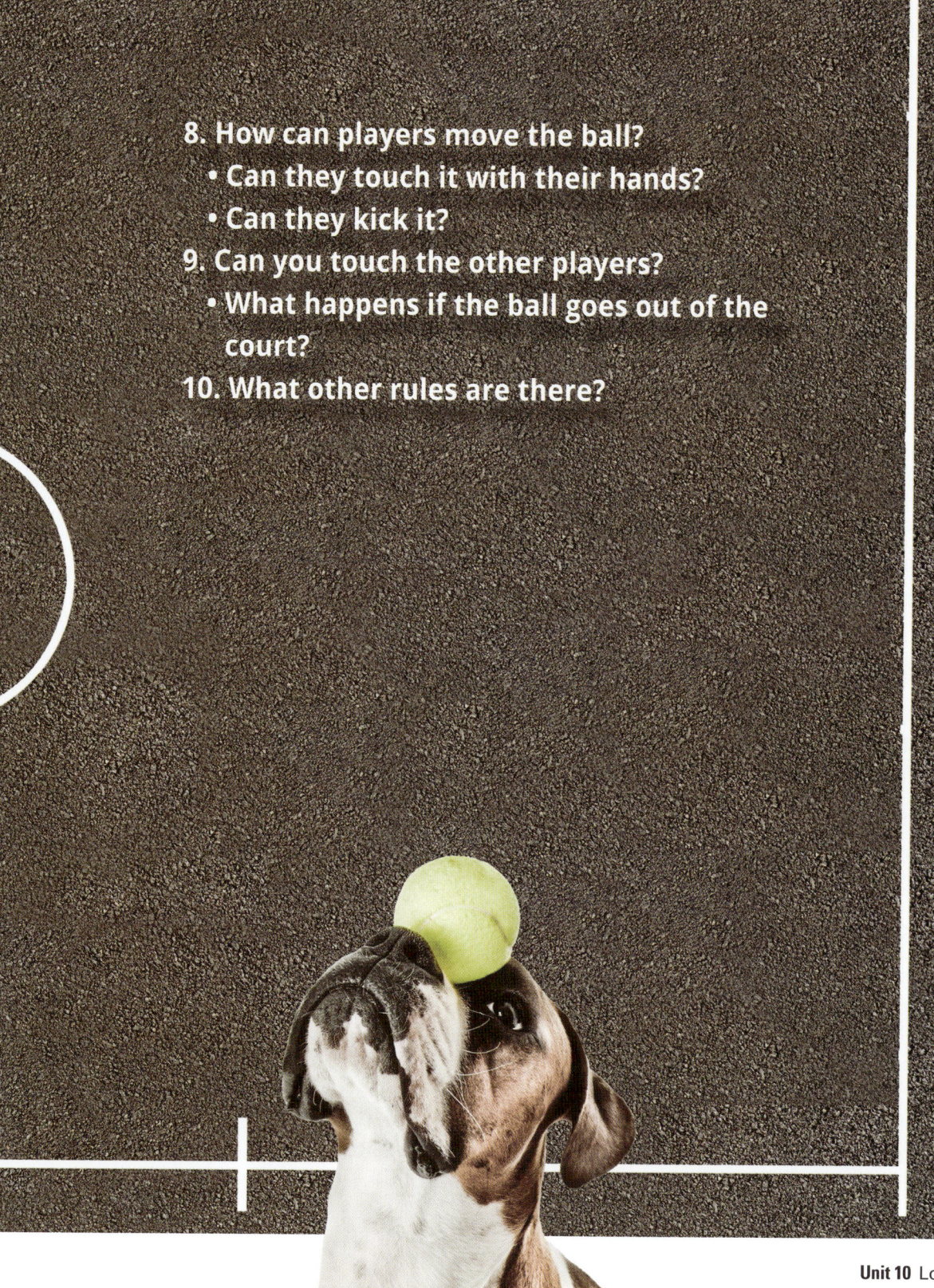

8. How can players move the ball?
   • Can they touch it with their hands?
   • Can they kick it?
9. Can you touch the other players?
   • What happens if the ball goes out of the court?
10. What other rules are there?

LISTENING DIALOGUES SLE 1C

UNIT 1 TRACK 2 and 3

David: Hey Dad, how's the class coming?

Henry: Don't ask! My brain just doesn't work this way.

David: Now, wait a second. Remember when I was learning how to play golf?

Henry: Yes, I remember. It took a while for you to get the hang of it.

David: That's right. Do you remember what I said after my first lesson?

Henry: (Laughing) You told me your body just didn't move that way. You said it was impossible.

David: And what did you tell me?

Henry: I told you that things took time. It's really easy for you now.

David: Right. It may take some time and practice, but you'll soon be coding like an old pro.

Henry: Or at least an old programmer!

UNIT 2 TRACK 4 and 5

Nick: Welcome to Queequeg coffee. How may I help you? Oh! Hi Mom. What can I get you?

Heather: Give me a coffee.

Nick: Sure. That'll be ten dollars.

Heather: What!? Ten dollars? That's outrageous!

Nick: I know, but it's cheaper if you say please.

Heather: Really? Okay, can I have a cup of coffee, please?

Nick: Why certainly! That will be five dollars.

Heather: Well, that's still pretty expensive.

Nick: Look at the menu Mom.

Heather: Oh! I see. Okay. Hello, may I please have a cup of coffee?

Nick: Yes you may. That will be one dollar.

Heather: Very cute. Could you put some milk in it for me?

Nick: I'd be happy to.

UNIT 3 TRACK 6 and 7

Bobby: It's so exciting Grandpa! I've never been in a cave before.

Henry: Yes, Bobby my boy, it is exciting. But first things first. There are some important safety considerations.

Bobby: Such as?

Henry: Watch your head! The ceiling can get pretty low, and you don't want a bruise.

Bobby: Okay. I'm excited to see the bats! Can I hold one?

Henry: Don't touch the bats Bobby, you could get bitten. Don't leave the group, so you don't get lost, and don't throw anything in the water.

Bobby: Why is that?

Henry: The cave is a very fragile place. Take pictures, but don't touch anything in the cave.

Bobby: It looks like it's our turn to go in!

Announcer: Okay gentlemen. Please buckle your seatbelts, and keep your arms inside the cart at all times. Here we go…

UNIT 4 TRACK 8 and 9

Nick: So how was your date with that guy Jack?

Ella: Don't ask. It was a disaster!

Nick: Really? His online profile made him look so unique.

Ella: Yeah, he SEEMED unique online, but in person, he was just weird.

Nick: Well, sometimes weird people can be fun if they're adventurous.

Ella: I dunno. He seemed adventurous when I talked to him on the phone. He said he liked hiking, but when we went to the mountains he was really cautious. He just wanted to hang out and look at the view.

Nick: Hmm. I know you want to meet someone who is adventurous, but maybe this guy has other good points. Didn't you say he was really hard-working?

Ella: He seemed hard-working because he said he wanted to stay in college for a few more years. He's actually just lazy. He doesn't want to graduate and find a job.

Nick: Does he have any good points?

Ella: We went to a movie after hiking, and he was really sensitive. He cried during the movie.

Nick: Uhhh. And that's a good thing?

Ella: I think so. Later we met some of my friends at a bar, and he was very outgoing. They liked him a lot.

Nick: That's good!

Ella: Yeah, but it just doesn't seem like he's the one.

UNIT 5 TRACK 10 and 11

Nick: Hello?

Henry: Hi, Nick?

Nick: Hey Grandpa! How's New York? Have you tried the pizza yet?

Henry: As a matter of fact, I just finished a slice at Giorgio's Pizza in the Financial District. I visited the Stock Exchange in the morning.

Nick: Wow great! What's next?

Henry: Well, that's why I'm calling you. I need to know how to get from Giorgio's to the Museum of American Finance.

Nick: Can't you just check on your phone?

Henry: Actually, I'm having trouble connecting. I don't think they have the Internet in New York.

Nick: Hmm. Maybe next year…

Henry: For now, can you check on your computer and explain it to me?

Nick: Okay. Are you inside Giorgio's now?

Henry: Yes.

Nick: Alright, go out the front door and go east on Beaver Street. Go across Broad Street.

Henry: Okay; straight on Beaver Street, across Broad Street, then what?

Nick: Then, turn left and go up William Street.

Henry: Turn left on William Street, okay. Do I turn at the next street?

Nick: No. No. No. Keep going on William Street until you get to Wall Street. Then, turn right on Wall Street. The museum is on Wall Street across from Extreme Gym. You can't miss it!

Henry: Okay. If I do, I'll call you back.

Nick: Right on.

UNIT 6 TRACK 12 and 13

Heather: Hi Honey. You're a little late. How was your day?

David: You'll never believe it! I was interviewed about a former student by the local news.

Heather: Wow! Who was the student?

David: He said the student's name was Karen Smith. He said she solved a famous math problem that no one has been able to do for hundreds of years.

Heather: That's really great. What did the interviewer ask you?

David: He asked me what I did to motivate my students.

Heather: What did you say?

David: I said I made math more interesting by showing students how it relates to their lives.

Heather: Great! What else did he ask?

David: He asked if Karen was a really talented student.

Heather: And?

David: I said honestly, I didn't remember her.

Heather: David!

UNIT 7 TRACK 14 and 15

Ella: There's something different about Grandma's lasagna this time, but I can't put my finger on it.

Nick: Is there less garlic than usual?

Ella: No, there's plenty of garlic in it.

Bobby: Are there different vegetables like carrots or celery?

Ella: No, that's not it. There are always carrots and celery in Grandma's sauce. She cuts them into small pieces, but they're always there.

Bobby: Yuck! Is she trying to poison me?

Ella: Oh come on, Bobby. There's nothing wrong with carrots and celery. If you don't like it, eat a peanut butter sandwich instead.

Nick: Wait a second. That's it. There's peanut butter in this! Grandma's been taking a Thai cooking class!

Ella: Is there such a thing as Thai lasagna?

Nick: I think Grandma just invented it. Lasagna with peanut sauce!

Bobby: I knew it. She really IS trying to poison us. There's no doubt.

Nick: Actually, I like it. Is there more?

UNIT 8 TRACK 16 and 17

Counselor: I have some great summer job opportunities available.

Nick: Which ones pay the best?

Counselor: Well, there's a summer job advertised here working as a tailor's assistant. That pays nicely.

Nick: I'd rather work outside than inside. I want to enjoy the summer.

Counselor: How about working as a clown at a kid's summer camp?

Nick: I'd rather not wear a costume.

Counselor: Okay. Would you rather work with animals or people? The city is looking for tour guides. The aquarium is looking for people to help with the dolphins.

Nick: Wow, dolphins! That sounds really cool. What's the pay?

Counselor: Well, it says here it's just an unpaid internship but that they provide lunch.

Nick: I'd prefer to make some money this summer.

Counselor: How about driving a machine around the golf course picking up golf balls? It's outside.

Nick: That sounds perfect. I'll apply now.

UNIT 9 TRACK 18 and 19

Ella: I'm going out to eat burgers at Bright Castle with my friends. Do you want me to bring you something?

Nick: Bright Castle? Don't forget your passport.

Ella: My passport? Why's that? I know it's close to the border, but it's not ACROSS the border.

Nick: I know, but there was this time when I tried to find Bright Castle with my friend, Harry.

Ella: What happened?

Nick: Well first, I went to hang out with Harry at his place, and we got super hungry.

Ella: Yeah? Then what?

Nick: Then, Harry and I went out looking for Bright Castle, but we took a wrong turn and drove into Mexico.

Ella: Uh-oh. What happened next?

Nick: Next, we tried to cross the border back into the United States, but Harry didn't have his passport.

Ella: Oops. So what did you do?

Nick: You won't believe it. I had to leave Harry in Mexico, drive back to his place, and get his passport. Then, I drove back, but I couldn't find him anywhere. Finally, I saw him sleeping in an ice cream shop.

Ella: Then did you go to Bright Castle?

Nick: NO! While he was waiting, Harry got hungry. So first, he ate some tacos on the street. Then, he went to a seafood restaurant. After that, he went to an ice cream place. Finally, he passed out. When we got back, he just wanted to go home.

Ella: So that's why you should always bring your passport to Bright Castle. Got it.

UNIT 10 TRACK 20 and 21

Heather: David, Could you help me for a minute?

David: Sure. What can I do for you?

Heather: I'm trying to remember what everyone is doing this summer, and I want to make sure I have it right.

David: Well, I'll just be driving to the golf course.

Heather: Henry is going fishing. How is he getting there?

David: He says he's taking a hot air balloon!

Heather: A what? Oh, never mind. And Ruth will be flying somewhere to do a charity run I'm sure.

David: That's correct. Isn't Ella going to be riding her bike to some kind of dance class?

Heather: They're Zumba classes dear. And yes, she really likes riding her new bike.

David: Bobby is headed to safari camp. He says they'll be taking…

Heather: Elephants to a tree house! I know. Sounds fabulous. What's Nick up to?

David: Well, he finally settled on a summer job. He's going to be cleaning some millionaire's yacht. So he'll be going wherever it takes him. How about you?

Heather: I have been asked to give a lecture at an architecture conference. I'll be taking the train.

David: Wow, really? That's fantastic news Hon!

GLOSSARY SLE 1C

A

Accordion *noun* a musical instrument with a keyboard and buttons — Unit 1
Adventurous *adjective* enjoying new, difficult, and/or dangerous things — Unit 4
Allergic *adjective* unable to eat, touch, or breathe something — Unit 6
Ambitious *adjective* strong desire to be successful — Unit 9
Amusing *adjective* humorous or entertaining — Unit 4
Appointment *noun* a scheduled meeting at a specific time — Unit 3
Assertive *adjective* strong and confident — Unit 4

B

Boundary *noun* limit; line marking the end of something — Unit 5

C

Carnival *noun* public festival celebrated before Lent; famous in Brazil — Unit 1
Caterpillar *noun* an insect that becomes a butterfly — Unit 2
Cautious *adjective* careful — Unit 4
Celebrity *noun* famous performer such as an entertainer or athlete — Unit 10
Cheated *adjective* tricked by someone — Unit 5
Clause *noun* a group of words with a subject and predicate — Unit 3
Clue *noun* helpful information — Unit 2
Coding *noun* writing computer programs — Unit 1
Compassionate *adjective* caring and kind — Unit 4
Compliment *noun* positive comment — Unit 1
Consequence *noun* bad result of an action — Unit 3
CPR (Cardio Pulmonary Respiration) *noun* emergency treatment for stopped heartbeat — Unit 1

D

Deadline *noun* the time set to finish a project — Unit 8
Decade *noun* a period of ten years — Unit 8
Deflect *verb* make something change direction — Unit 7
Diaper *noun* piece of cloth or plastic, worn on the bottom by babies — Unit 1
Dictator *noun* a ruler with total control of a country's people — Unit 3
Drown *verb* to die under water — Unit 7
Durable *adjective* strong; hard to break — Unit 2
Durian *noun* fruit from Southeast Asia — Unit 1

E

Exaggerate *verb* describe something as more than the reality — Unit 8

F

Fable *noun* a traditional story, usually with animal characters and a moral — Unit 9

Facial *noun* beauty treatment for the face — Unit 5
Fare *noun* amount charged for a ride — Unit 5
Fashion statement *idiom* an item of clothing that expresses a lifestyle — Unit 5
Flexible *adjective* able to handle change comfortably — Unit 4
Fluent *adjective* able to communicate like a native — Unit 1
Frustrate *verb* to cause someone stress due to difficulty or hardship — Unit 4
Fusion *adjective* mixing of two or more things — Unit 2

G

Gamble *verb* playing games with the chance of losing or winning money — Unit 3
Garbage dump *noun* a place that gathers large amounts of trash — Unit 5
Germs *noun* viruses or bacteria — Unit 3
Glamorous *adjective* stylish and beautiful — Unit 2
Gossip *verb* talk about other people — Unit 6
Grouchy *adjective* bad tempered, in a mood to complain — Unit 4

H

Haunted *adjective* having ghosts — Unit 3
Hideout *noun* a place where somebody is hiding — Unit 5
Hold your breath *collocation* wait and not breathe — Unit 6

I

Imitation *adjective* copied — Unit 2
Imperative *adjective* ordering; making somebody do something — Unit 3
Impression *noun* an opinion or feeling — Unit 5
Impulsive *adjective* acting without thinking — Unit 9
Introverted *adjective* shy; keeping thoughts and feelings inside — Unit 4
Iron *verb* press a hot piece of metal on cloth to make it smooth — Unit 1

J

K

Kick out *phrasal verb* to send somebody away — Unit 5
Kidnap *verb* take away by force — Unit 3

L

Landmarks *noun* famous places — Unit 5
Lava *noun* hot liquid from a volcano — Unit 7
Leash *noun* long piece of cloth used to hold a dog by the neck — Unit 3
Littering *noun* throwing trash on the ground — Unit 3
Logs *noun* cut trees — Unit 7

M

Manhole *noun* a hole in the street used for underground work — Unit 7

Maven *noun* an expert — Unit 1
Mean *adjective* unkind — Unit 8
Mellow *adjective* very calm — Unit 4
Memorize *verb* to remember something — Unit 1
Moral of the story *noun* lesson taught by the story — Unit 9

N

National anthem *noun* official song of a country — Unit 1
Natto *noun* Japanese fermented soybeans — Unit 1
Negotiation *noun* a conversation used to find an agreement — Unit 8
Neighbor *noun* a person that lives next to you — Unit 6
Newborn *adjective* a baby that has recently been born — Unit 1
Number cruncher *noun* a person who works well with numbers and data — Unit 8

O

Obstacle *noun* a thing that makes it hard to move in one direction — Unit 7
On the town *idiom* at a city's nightlife locations such as restaurants and bars — Unit 3
Outdoorsy *adjective* having a style matching outdoor activities — Unit 4
Outgoing *adjective* friendly; not shy — Unit 4

P

Passive *adjective* lacking positive action — Unit 6
Penalty *noun* an official punishment — Unit 3
Pessimistic *adjective* having negative ideas — Unit 4
Portable *adjective* easy to carry — Unit 2
Prohibition *noun* stopping somebody from doing something — Unit 3
Propose *verb* ask to marry — Unit 5
Punctual *adjective* on time; not late — Unit 4 and Unit 8
Pushup *noun* exercise pushing the body up from the floor with the arms — Unit 1

Q

Quack *verb* make a sound like a duck — Unit 6

R

Reserved *adjective* polite; not aggressive — Unit 4
Resistant *adjective* not easily damaged by something — Unit 2
Résumé *noun* a summary of skills and education — Unit 8
Retirement home *noun* a place for elderly people who can no longer live alone — Unit 5
Revolting *adjective* creating feelings of disgust — Unit 4
Rotary *adjective* turning — Unit 2

S

Safari *noun* a trip to see animals — Unit 1
Scenic *adjective* having a pretty view — Unit 2
Self-centered *adjective* not caring about other people — Unit 4

Sense of direction *collocation* not caring about other people — Unit 4
Sentimental *adjective* affected by emotion easily — Unit 4
Settle down *phrasal verb* get married and start a family — Unit 1
Sew *verb* use a needle and thread to make or fix clothing — Unit 1
Shopping spree *noun* a short period of spending a lot of money — Unit 2
Siblings *noun* brothers and sisters — Unit 6
Significant other *noun* husband, wife, or long term partner — Unit 6
Slippery *adjective* easy to slide on a surface — Unit 3
Smoke detector *noun* a device that sets off an alarm when it is aware of smoke — Unit 3
Soothing *adjective* able to make calm — Unit 2
Soul mate *noun* another person that is the ideal match for a relationship — Unit 7
Souvenir *noun* something bought to remind you of a place — Unit 5
Spreadsheet *noun* document with information in rows and columns; calculates numbers — Unit 1
Stingy *adjective* not liking to spend money — Unit 4
Straightforward *adjective* very honest and clear — Unit 6
Swear *verb* say bad words — Unit 3

T

Thrifty *adjective* tight with money — Unit 4
Timid *adjective* afraid; not confident — Unit 4
Turnstile *noun* entrance gate with metal bars that move in a circle — Unit 5
TV personality *noun* someone who appears regularly on TV — Unit 4
Twirl *verb* turn, spin — Unit 1

U

Under pressure *idiom* feeling stressed to finish something — Unit 8
Unique *adjective* special; not ordinary — Unit 4
Unisex *adjective* used by both males and females — Unit 2
Uptight *adjective* nervous and sensitive — Unit 4

V

Vegetarian restaurant *noun* a restaurant for people who do not eat meat — Unit 5
Verbal *adjective* with spoken words — Unit 3

W

White lies *idiom* lies that are told to protect someone's feelings — Unit 6
Work out *phrasal verb* exercise — Unit 1

X

Y

Z